I0058123

Growing The Money Tree

Financial Freedom` One Leaf At A Time
JOHN SVAZIC

ARM Trading Press

Published in Canada
Typeset with the LATEX Documentation System

Dedication

To Tammy - Thank you for standing by me and showing me the dreams worth reaching for. You are my muse.

To Jackson and Hannah - Thank you for showing me what true perseverance is, even before either of you could say the word. You are my determination.

To Mary - Thank you for your love and showing me what an iron will looks like. You are my focus.

Acknowledgments

I want to thank all my friends, family, acquaintances and strangers for all the help in making this book happen. From proofreaders to fact checkers, reviewers and critics, I thank you. No journey is successfully traveled alone, and this book is no exception. Without the support of a great many, this book would not have become a reality. Each of you has my enduring thanks and everlasting respect for the assistance you have provided. There are not enough words to thank each of you individually, but I do offer my sincerest gratitude and best wishes in pursuing your own goals in life.

I also want to give a special thank you to Tony Serban and Peter Sosnowski. Thank you gentlemen for your faith and support.

Contents

Disclaimer

This book is designed to provide personal information and experiences on trading on the foreign exchange market using artificial intelligence techniques. It is sold with the understanding that the publisher and author are not engaged in rendering legal, accounting or other professional services. If legal or other expert assistance is required, the services of a competent professional should be sought. It is not the purpose of this manual to reprint all the information that is otherwise available to authors and/or publishers, but instead to complement, amplify and supplement other texts. You are urged to read all the available material, learn as much as possible about the foreign exchange market, and tailor the information to your individual needs.

Investing in any type of environment, be it foreign exchange, stocks, bonds, etc, has risk associated with it. This book is about my personal experiences with some of these investment types and it is not intended to be used as a step-by-step guide for your own financial needs. Always use your own best judgement before you invest your money. Every effort has been made to make this manual as complete and as accurate as possible. However, there may be mistakes, both typographical and in content.

Disclaimer

The purpose of this manual is to educate and entertain. The author and publisher shall have neither liability nor responsibility to any person or entity with respect to any loss or damage caused, or alleged to have been caused, directly or indirectly, by the information contained in this book.

Introduction

Hello, my name is John and I want to work at Starbucks. Yes, you read that right. I don't want to have a huge mansion, a giant yacht, 20 cars or anything else that is normally attributed to the wealthy. I just want to live a simple, but comfortable, life. I like talking to people. I like sharing ideas. I like to get out and do things. Working as a Barista at my local Starbucks seems like a nice change from the corporate jungle I'm used to now. Also knowing that you don't need the job you have makes that job more fulfilling in a way. You are essentially doing it out of love for the job, and not for the pay from that job. For me it is being a Barista at Starbucks, but for others it may be something else completely.

So how exactly am I planning on fulfilling this "dream"? Well, that's what this book is all about. I'm growing a money tree. *Money tree* is what I call my personal investment and retirement plan. If you have a financial advisor then you're likely also growing your own money tree. Maybe it's not growing at the rate you want, or maybe you wish you had a bit more control over how it grows or is shaped. That's how I felt when I started growing my money tree, and that's why I wrote this book.

The Foreign Exchange Market

I want to share with you my experiences in growing part of my money tree by trading currencies on the foreign exchange market.

I say "part" since I want my money tree to be healthy, but one does not grow a tree by planting it and pouring lots of water on it. You need sunlight, fertilizer and pruning as well. I love the foreign exchange market, but I do not rely on it for my only source of investment income.

Diversification is key in any sort of investment strategy, and the foreign exchange market is usually one method that people tend to overlook. I think it is an interesting investment opportunity that has a large potential for reward, albeit with more risk. However, since anyone with a computer can participate, it makes for an interesting opportunity I'll see if you want to help your own money tree along.

In Chapter 11 you'll read about my early experiences in trading the foreign exchange market. It has very little to do with growing a money tree, but it should help you understand where my mind-set was when I first stumbled across it.

Artificial Intelligence

My love for artificial intelligence (AI) goes back to when I was a student in university. I went to my school's bookstore regularly to find the perfect pencil, see what books were being used for other courses, and because I loved to read, to see what was new. There was only a small section dedicated to AI, but it was good enough for me. Keep in mind that this was before the days of Amazon, so I had to make do! Nevertheless, I was fascinated by these books. I bought a number of them and started to learn the differences between expert systems and neural networks, with the latter being what captured most of my attention. The idea of being able to design a system that could recognize patterns was incredible! Neural networks are used for things like voice recognition, time series prediction, and classifying data.

Neural networks are fun, but there is as much of an art to them as there is a science. The algorithms for neural networks are pretty well known, so writing them into a program is not necessarily hard. There are two tricks to being able to use a neural network properly; the first is being able to format the input and the second is being able to interpret the output from them. There has been a lot of research done over the last 30+ years trying to use artificial intelligence systems such as neural networks and expert systems to formulate strategies and predict the stock market. I think every grad student who studies AI thinks about striking it rich at least once - but not everyone is successful. When I started to look into AI in general (and neural networks in particular), I did not know enough about the stock market to care about trying to predict it. I was more interested in the application of neural networks to find patterns in all sorts of things. Over the years I have used neural networks for lots of different projects, my favorite one was trying to find the best packet size for file transfers over a heterogeneous network topology. It sounds fancy, but it was the equivalent of trying to balance a board on a ball. I never did finish that one, since it was for a work project that stopped after I left that particular organization.

A few years ago I started hearing more about evolutionary algorithms, a "new" branch of AI that included things like genetic algorithms (GA) and genetic programming (GP) as some of its subconcepts. GAs caught my attention because of their simplicity. Essentially they "grow" a solution to a problem by starting with a whole bunch of potential solutions and testing them against the problem. New solutions are generated through breeding, mutation, or elitism where some of the original solutions are kept unchanged. This process repeats over and over, generation over generation, until you either find an ideal solution or you decide to stop looking for new solutions. All of this will be covered in more detail in the *Genetic Algorithms* part of the book. Basically if you have a way to measure how "good" a solution is, then genetic algorithms are a great way to find a solution to a particular problem. Think of it like a hybrid plant that is cross bred with another plant to make it less susceptible to disease. I followed this approach in the hopes of finding new successful trading strategies for the foreign exchange market. I'll explore more of how I did this later in the book.

Planting The Tree

This book is more than just about foreign exchange and genetic algorithms. At first I wanted to share with the world how I combined them to make something unique, interesting and profitable, but I realized that this was just one part of my investment portfolio. I was investing in a way that would give me the ability to live my life comfortably, with complete financial freedom. I was *growing a money tree*.

Growing a money tree is about the desire to find financial freedom so you can live your life and enjoy it to the fullest. Trading the foreign exchange market is one part of my money tree, but it is not the only part. This book will focus mostly on the foreign exchange market and how to trade it, but I do cover some other investment options that you should consider.

Who This Book Is For

If you are curious about what genetic algorithms are and how they work, you may find this book a little easier to read than some of the other more academic books on the subject. If you want to learn more about the foreign exchange market and how you can get started, this book is for you. If you want to learn about what my view of a money tree is and how I am growing mine, this book is for you.

If you are a hard-core foreign exchange trader, if you have a PhD in artificial intelligence, if you want to get rich quick, this is not the book you are looking for.

My target audience is the average person who has some money they want to invest on the side, and they want to try something new. I don't recommend that anyone put all their money into a single investment type, be it stocks, mutual funds, foreign exchange, or anything else. I think everyone should have their own "guilty pleasure" investment; investing in Coca-Cola™or in my case the foreign exchange market. Add some extra nutrients to your money tree and have fun with it. If you are passionate about it, you may be able to make yourself a decent profit.

Growing a money tree is as much about finding financial freedom and independence as it is about having fun and experiencing a sense of control over your financial needs. If these ideas appeal to you, then you have found the right book.

How This Book Is Organized

Part I will mainly cover the foreign exchange market. I introduce what the foreign exchange market is, the terminology it uses, some tools you can use to spot trends, and give an example of how you can use these tools to make actual trades. I'll also cover some other popular investment options and give my own view of them, all in the hopes of giving you more tools to help cultivate your money tree.

Part II gives a brief introduction to genetic algorithms and how to use them to come up with strategies for trading the foreign exchange market. By the end of Part II, you will have a good working knowledge of what genetic algorithms are, how they work and how they can be used to help find successful strategies for trading the foreign exchange market. I will also offer some thoughts and advice based on personal experiences I have learned over the years.

Part III is where the majority of my personal story is told. I'll tell you all about my early days learning how to trade in the foreign exchange market, what I did well and what failed for me, how I decided to start using genetic algorithms for trading strategies and some reflections on why I'm growing my money tree.

So let's get started! Warren Buffett once said:

Someone's sitting in the shade today because someone planted a tree a long time ago.

Let's get planting.

Part I

Plant The Money Tree

CHAPTER 1

Debt And Taxes

I bet you have some goals in your life. Maybe you want a bigger house, maybe you want to own a vacation home. Maybe you just want to retire. Maybe you just want to be happy.

There is a common belief that if you have *more* then you will have a better life. But more of *what* exactly? Money? Power? A well placed Scarface one-liner?

Most people, even the rich, want more money and so they have a goal to increase their personal wealth. But what does that tell you? What it tells me is the desire for wealth is never ending. I mean, how will I ever be happy if the people I view as wealthy are still looking for more money themselves?

That's when I realized that a more worthwhile goal is *more time*. Time to spend with my family, time to pursue my interests. Who wouldn't want more time to live their life? Isn't that why people want to retire?

The Retired Businessman And The Fisherman

Some of you may have heard of the story of the businessman who retired to an island and the fisherman he meets there. I won't repeat the story verbatim here, but I will give you the gist of the story.

A businessman retires to a coastal village and spots a fisherman who comes in with some fish. When the businessman asks about how long it took to fish, the fisherman says "Not very long at all." So the businessman asks why he did not fish longer to get more fish. The reply from the fisherman was that he sleeps in and he had enough fish to help his family and that he spends the rest of his day playing with his children, spending time with his wife, visiting his friends in the city as they sip wine and play the guitar. The businessman goes on to tell the fisherman about a great plan he has to expand his fishing trips, grow a great empire of fishing trawlers and after 20-30 years make millions and retire a wealthy man! The fisherman then asks what he would do after he retires, to which the businessman replies spending time with his family, sleeping in, drinking wine with his friends and playing a guitar.

At this point the fisherman asks: "Is this not what I am doing already?"

Retirement, financial freedom, not having to work anymore and having more time to yourself. Call it what you will, that is the goal of growing a money tree. Of course there is something that can stunt the growth of any money tree and we need to cover that first - let's look at *debt*.

1.1 Understanding Debt

There are a lot of books about personal investing and financial planning that completely ignore debt. Debt is bad, but chances are that you have some. In this section I want to talk about the different types of debt. I also want to cover why some types of debt shouldn't prevent you from growing a money tree while others should be addressed well before you plan that first seed.

1.1.1 What Is Debt?

So what exactly is debt? Paraphrasing the definition a bit, debt is when you owe something to something or someone else. For the remainder of this book I will define debt as being money owed to an individual or institution, be it from a credit card, mortgage, loan, or a lease owed to a bank, credit card company, government, loan shark, etc.

Being completely debt free is the ideal goal, but it can be a difficult one to attain if you did not start this journey early enough in life. Some debt can be seen as necessary, such as mortgage debt. Other debt can be avoided if we are smart, like credit card debt. Unfortunately as a society, we tend not to realize the consequences of the rash and impulsive decisions we make that can lead to debt. So what can we do? First thing's first, let me break down debt into *good debt* and *bad debt*, since there is a difference.

1.1.2 Good versus Bad Debt

Is there such a thing as good debt? In my opinion I believe there is. It may be easier to explain if I give you my definition of what bad debt is first.

Bad debt is any type of monetary debt that is forcing you to pay extraordinary fees for having the "privilege" of using someone else's money. Things like credit cards, payday loans and even some mortgages fall into this definition. High interest rates, painful payment

5

schedules or anything else that makes you face a dreadful job day-in and day-out in order to pay a debt back are signs that this is a bad debt.

Credit Cards Redux

Credit cards are the devil as far as I'm concerned. When used properly they can be useful, but most people who have them do not use them properly. Most people use their credit card, accumulate debt and then ride that debt for *years* before paying it off completely. That is a bad thing.

Let me shed a different light on why holding on to credit card debt for longer than necessary is a bad idea. What would you prefer? Would you rather make a 10% or a 20% return on your investments? 20% of course! I know I sure would! Making twice as much money is always better, right?

Would you like to take a guess at what happens when people take their time paying off their credit card debt? The average APR for a consumer credit card in North America is 19.9%, so people who carry a credit card balance end up paying nearly 20% more to the bank in interest rather than having that extra 20% help *them* make money via investments.

Good debt is any debt where the interest rate on the debt is lower than the interest rate for the returns you are making from any investments. Things like first-mortgages[1] and secured lines of credit are examples of *good debt*.

---

[1]Second and third mortgages often have much higher interest rates, and as such I would classify them as *bad debt*.

When Good Debt Goes Bad

Just because I consider a first mortgage to be a *good* debt doesn't mean that you should get the biggest one available so you can get the biggest house on the market! This is a bad idea, since you still need to *pay that debt back*! There are a lot of factors to consider, so don't jump in over your head. The housing crisis in the United States that started in mid-2008 is a great example of what can happen if you take on more good debt than you can handle.

Be smart, don't be greedy, and have a budget before you decide to increase on any good debt you already have.

Debt is a reality in most peoples lives. It can take on many forms; from mortgages to car loans, from spousal support to outstanding credit card balances. If you have a lot of *bad debt* in your life, then please speak with a credit councilor before you try to grow a money tree. Get rid of that bad debt completely before you begin. It may take you a little longer to get started, but it will be worth so much more in the end.

Personal debt is a complicated and emotional topic for most people. If you find yourself in a position with a lot of debt and you are struggling to pay your bills or are just "scraping by", then please seek outside help before you start trying to grow your money tree. Beware of single-solution credit councilors. If you need to speak with someone, try to find an organization that will give you multiple options to deal with your debt. Single-solution providers may not have your best interests in mind. Debt problems are complex and as it tends to be with most complex things in our lives, there is no single answer that works for everyone.

With the debt discussion out of the way, we can start focusing on growing a money tree for my fictional friend *Bob*.

1.2 What Is Your *Real* Income?

Meet Bob. Bob is my fictional friend living somewhere in Ontario, Canada[2]. Bob is single, has a small house and wants to grow his money tree. Ultimately Bob wants to retire and live life to the fullest. He also wants to work at a Starbucks part time because he likes the idea of going out and meeting new people. However, Bob's problem is that he's not sure how much money he needs his money tree to make for him in order to quit his current job. Let's see how we can help Bob realize his dream.

Back in 2010, the median total income before tax for an individual in Canada[3] was just shy of $30,000. Bob is making a bit more than that, bringing in $60,000 per year with his current job.

Bob's story is not uncommon, except for the Starbucks bit - that's a little odd if you ask me. In order to help Bob find out how much money he needs his money tree to make for him, we need to know where Bob's money is going now.

---

[2]While Bob lives in Ontario, Canada, his story is pretty generic. I put Bob in Ontario in order to use accurate tax rates, but the ideas and concepts I put forward for the rest of the chapter can easily be applied to anyone else in a similar situation to Bob.

[3]http://www.statcan.gc.ca/tables-tableaux/sum-som/l01/cst01/famil105a-eng.htm

1.2.1 Break Down the Income

Bob is pretty happy with his quality of life. Sure he could always use some more money, but when it boils right down to it Bob is content when he's at home. What Bob wants now is to cut his work hours while maintaining his quality of life.

The first thing we're going to do is figure out exactly what Bob's "take home" (or *net*) income is per year. I'll start by breaking down the standard deductions that are taken off Bob's income by the Canadian government[4]:

- Approximately $10,210 in Federal income tax
- Approximately $4,805 in Provincial income tax
- Approximately $2,307 in Canada Pension Plan (CPP) contributions
- Approximately $840 for Employment Insurance (EI) contributions

So after all these deductions, Bob has a net income of $41,838 per year. Naturally there are additional refunds and other tax actions that apply, so let me round up slightly and say that Bob is essentially working with $42,000 of net income for the year. This works out to $42,000 \div 12 = \$3,500$ per month.

1.2.2 Knowing What You Need - Build A Budget

Let's whip up a quick budget for Bob using some standard expenses that he has in his life. Table 1.1 provides a list of Bob's monthly expenses, including some extra cash for general spending.

Bob's budget may look a little different than yours, but at least it gives us a sense of where he stands financially each month. This is useful, since it looks like Bob has roughly $1,000 left over each

---

[4] Revenue Canada Tax Rates 2012 - http://www.cra-arc.gc.ca/tx/ndvdls/fq/txrts-eng.html

Mortgage[a]	$985
Car Payment	$250
House Insurance	$75
Car Insurance	$100
Heating	$75
Electricity	$100
Fuel for Car	$200
Groceries	$500
Cell Phone, Television, Internet	$150
"Spending Money"	$1030

Table 1.1: A Simple Budget For Bob

---

[a]$150,000 mortgage with a 4.99% annual interest rate over a 20 year amortization period.

month. Bob budgets $500 each month for entertainment and other expenses, with the remaining $500 going towards his money tree.

1.2.3 Be The Barista - Identify The Path Forward

One of Bob's goals is to be a Barista at his local Starbucks. A little odd, but that's okay since it makes him happy. So what does Bob need to do in order to reach it? First Bob needs to make sure he can maintain his quality of life. We have a plan for what he needs monthly, so we'll start with this bare necessity.

If we exclude the payments to help his money tree, Bob needs about $3,000 per month to keep him in his current lifestyle (or $36,000 per year). Even though Bob wants to work at Starbucks, he's only looking for about 10 - 15 hours of work per week. A Barista at Starbucks stands to make roughly $12 per hour, or roughly $12.5 \times 12 = 150 per week. We'll base that on the average number of hours per week that Bob would work, which is $(10 + 15) \div 2 = 12.5$.

Bob also wants to be able to travel through the year - he plans on taking 6 weeks each year, but not all at once. He doesn't expect to be paid for all that time off, so he needs to account for that. With 52 weeks per year, this puts Bob's gross annual income from Starbucks at around $150 \times 46 = \$6,900$. After income taxes (Federal and Provincial), CPP and EI contributions, Bob stands to make roughly $\$5,200$ per year while working as a Barista.

Now that Bob knows what he can expect to make from Starbucks, he can start planning on what he needs from his money tree. Since the Starbucks that Bob wants to work at is closer to his home than his current job and the fact that he likely won't be driving as far every day, Bob figures that the gas savings alone should let him cut the minimum amount he needs to keep his lifestyle to $\$35,000$ per year instead of $\$36,000$. Subtracting his Starbucks earnings, Bob is looking to have his money tree earn him at least $\$30,000$ per year[5]. Bob is already starting to daydream about all those lattes...

1.2.4 Enter The Tax Man

Bob's current income tax rate is about 25%. Factor in his CPP and EI deductions and the total amount that Bob pays the government works out to nearly 30% of his gross salary! That's quite the cut!

Bob does want to work at Starbucks though, and he is willing to take these cuts on his Starbucks salary. However since he is not making as much, the amount the government takes from him is less, working out to be roughly 24.6%.

Here's where things get interesting. In Canada, things like Canadian dividend earnings[6] and foreign exchange income is taxed at a lower rate than income tax! Foreign exchange profits are taxed at the capital gains rate, which states that 50% of the earnings will be taxed at the individual tax rate. So assuming that Bob was working at

---

[5]After tax, of course
[6]Covered in Section 7.4.1.

Starbucks and he made $30,000 in foreign exchange gains to sustain his lifestyle, $15,000 of his gains would be taxed at his personal tax rate, which would be 24.6%.

Taxes make my head hurt so I'll keep it simple. Table 1.2 shows what Bob's net income would be after paying taxes and other deductions if he had made $30,000 while working full time.

Gross Salary	$30,000.00
Federal Tax (15%)	−$4,500.00
Provincial Tax (5.05%)	−$1,515.00
CPP (4.95%)	−$1,485.00
EI (1.83%)	−$549.00
Net	$21,951.00

Table 1.2: Income Tax Breakdown of $30,000 Earned While Employed

And now let's see what Bob's net income would be if the same amount came from foreign exchange income, which is taxed at the *capital gains* tax rate. Table 1.3 gives us this breakdown.

Gross Income	$30,000.00
Federal Tax (15%)	−$2,250.00
Provincial Tax (5.05%)	−$757.50
Net	$26,992.50

Table 1.3: Income Tax Breakdown of $30,000 Earned From Capital Gains

Foreign exchange income is considered a capital gain and thus only 50% of the income is taxed at the individuals income tax rate. There is a savings of over $5,000 when the income is coming from investment income like foreign exchange trading! That's quite the difference and definitely not something to take lightly. Of course other investment vehicles offer other benefits. I will cover some of them in Chapter 7.

Tax laws change constantly, and I do not profess to be a tax guru. The information that I have included here is based on my interpretation of the tax laws from 2012 for an individual living in Ontario, Canada. Tax rates and laws will vary from country-to-country, province-to-province and state-to-state. Be smart and use a local tax professional to assist you with your taxes. They can help you keep the most amount of money from your money tree and from any employment income should you wish to keep working like Bob.

I didn't go into what tax exemptions or other loopholes Bob could have used for his income in this chapter. Again, a tax professional can help you maximize your returns and thus increase the amount of "found money" you can receive at income tax time.

1.3 Summary

Bob is pretty excited. Not only does he now know what he needs to survive, he's pretty sure that he can make his living. Also considering that the tax rate on investment income is much lower than his income tax for working, he has high hopes that he can reach his dream of freedom much, much sooner.

In the next chapter I want to introduce you to my investment vehicle of choice for building my personal money tree - the *foreign exchange market*.

CHAPTER 2

What Is Forex?

Forex is the (commonly used) short name for the *foreign exchange market*. Simple enough, so let's begin with an equally simple question: what exactly *is* the Forex? The Forex is a market where people buy and sell *currencies*.

While the Forex is similar to the stock market in that you buy and sell something to make a profit, there are some key differences. First you are not buying or selling a *share* in a company, you are buying or selling currency. If you have ever traveled to another country that uses a different currency than your own, then you likely had to exchange your home country's currency for the local currency of the country you visited. Congratulations! You have already participated in the Forex! You just happened to use a currency exchange booth, a bank or some other money exchanger rather than a broker. Converting one currency for another currency is exactly what happens when you make a trade in the Forex.

2.1   The Forex Market

I want to take a step back and look at what the stock market is and how it works. At a very high level the stock market is a listing of public companies that allow you to buy shares of those companies. If you want to make some money, you generally would sell[1] those shares for more than you purchased them for and hopefully make a profit. You may be aware that there are multiple stock markets throughout the world, such as the New York Stock Exchange (NYSE), NASDAQ, Toronto Stock Exchange (TSX), Nikkei, Hang Seng and about a dozen others spread throughout a dozen other countries.

Each of these stock markets operate in their own respective time zones with their own companies, with some large international companies being listed on more than one stock exchange. Each stock market is independent, so even if the same company is listed on two different exchanges, they are essentially independent stocks. For example, it is common to see a company being traded in both the NASDAQ and the TSX if they are a Canadian technology company. So assuming I buy one share of the company on the TSX, that does not translate in me being able to sell that share on the NASDAQ. They both trade the same company, but the shares are essentially tied to the market where they are purchased.

The Forex is different. First of all, there is just one market. That's it. Just one global market that is open starting every Sunday at 10:00 Greenwich Mean Time (GMT), 24 hours per day, until Friday at 22:00 GMT. So while most stock markets are, on average, opened for trading for 6.5 consecutive hours per day, the Forex is open for 134 *consecutive hours per week*. Quite the difference!

The Forex market is actually a global decentralized market. That means it does not operate under any single organization like the stock exchanges I listed previously do. For example the NYSE is owned and

---

[1]Of course dividend shares are another way to make money, but not all companies offer dividends.

operated by the *NYSE Euronext* corporation[2], which is based in New York City, New York.

Being decentralized, the Forex uses financial centers to help facilitate the main trading in the markets amongst the various players. There are financial centers in Sydney, Tokyo, Frankfurt, London and New York that help drive the Forex, and the overlap between the time zones where these financial centers are located is what helps keep the market open for so long.

So who exactly trades on the Forex? Just about anyone and everyone! Banks, central banks, commercial companies, investment firms and individuals like you and me are just some of the traders on the Forex. The Forex market is huge, and I mean really huge. To put it into perspective, in 2010 the NYSE (which is the biggest stock market in the world) had an average daily value of $153 billion US. The average daily value traded on the Forex for the same year was roughly $3.98 *trillion* US! There are a lot of traders working on the Forex every day, and there's always room for one more.

We talk about the Forex being used to trade currencies, but what currencies do we mean? Quite literally all the currencies in the world. For traders who trade on the Forex, there are major currencies they like to work with. These major currencies represent the most *liquid*, or most frequently traded, currencies and thus make them a must-know for any currency trader. Table 2.1 lists these major currencies along with their associated symbols.

There are other currencies outside these major ones that are known as *exotic currencies*. Some examples include:

- South African Rand (ZAR)

- Israeli Shekel (ILS)

- Brazilian Real (BZR)

- South African Rand (ZAR)

---

[2]They actually run multiple securities exchanges, but you get the idea.

Currency Name	Symbol
United States Dollar	USD
Eurozone Euro	EUR
Japanese Yen	JPY
British Pound	GBP
Swiss Franc	CHF
Canadian Dollar	CAD
Australian Dollar	AUD
New Zealand Dollar	NZD

Table 2.1: Major Forex Currencies

...and so on, but I won't be covering any of these exotic currencies in detail. Exotic currencies can either be incredibly *volatile*, meaning that their prices change rather quickly and these changes can be difficult to predict, or they do not have a lot of *trade volume* meaning they are not traded as much as the majors..

Even if you have an opportunity to trade these exotic currencies, I would not recommend it for any new trader. I can draw on a personal experience here - early in my Forex trading career I lost a good chunk of my account balance by trading the South African Rand (ZAR). It seemed like a good idea at the time since the price trends seemed to be predictable. However the trade volume was too low and the volatility was way too high. My broker was issuing margin calls against my orders, closing them out before I could turn a profit. Before I knew it, I lost most of my account balance! My order sizes were wrong, I was over leveraged, I went *Long* when I should have gone *Short*, my SL triggers were non-existent and I was blindly making trades without following the trend.

What exactly did I just say? A whole lot of gibberish? This is the type of paragraph you could expect to read in some other Forex books that expect you to know the terminology. I include it here on purpose to give you a glimpse into what you will learn in Chapter 3. I promise this will all make sense in time.

Where Currencies Live

While not critical, it is important to keep in mind that each major currency has a relationship with the financial center to the country in which it is based. For example, the USD is tied with the New York center, and the EUR is tied with the Frankfurt financial center. What this means is there is generally a lot more activity during the hours when these centers are operating, which means more movement (and therefore the potential for more profit) with these currencies. If you are looking at price trends and you notice some wild activity in the prices, you may want to see if the price changes overlap with the hours of one of these markets.

Some veteran traders swear by trading these financial center hours, but my experience has been to trade all hours equally using movement indicators I will show you later. You may not be maximizing profits like they are trying to do, but you can still make a nice profit.

So now that you can see how huge the market is, the next question is how do you get started? Much like the stock market, you need to find a *broker* that will help you make your trades.

2.2 Brokers

A *broker* is your entry point into the market, allowing you to perform trades on the Forex. This is similar to how stocks and commodities work, where you have a broker act as a middle-man to execute trades on your behalf. Much like with stock brokers, not all Forex brokers are created equal. You will want to make sure you do your fair share of research before you settle on one. Some key items I would consider when looking for a broker would include:

- Is the broker regulated by a government agency?
- Does the broker have a good reputation?
- Does the broker offer a practice account?
- How easy is their trading platform to use? account?

Of all the points above, regulation is the most important one. Regulation ensures a broker is not a scam who will take your money and run. Regulation also helps ensure the broker won't use false feeds, tricking you into making trades that lose. Regulation won't stop a broker from cheating you, but it does help. Do your research and try a few out if they offer practice accounts.

A close second is the trading platform itself. Some brokers offer their own trading system, others use something like *MetaTrader*[3] as their default trading platform software. I'm not a huge fan of Meta-Trader myself, but I do like some of the other trading platforms that are provided by brokers themselves. You need to be comfortable with what this interface looks like though, since you will be spending a lot of time using it. If it is too complex, or lacks some of the features you want to use, then look elsewhere. Most brokers will offer a few training video to help you get started, so don't give up too easily. Try a few out and find one that works for you.

When you first start out, a practice account is vital. This will let you practice your trading strategy with real data, all without risking a penny. Most brokers offer this service for free, but some will only offer it for a trial period they extend only after you open a live account. I personally prefer to take my time evaluating any new broker, and I hate being rushed into anything!

Reputation for a broker is important as well. Be careful when you are reading reviews and you see negative comments. Try to get a sense for where the person is coming from. Are they complaining because

---

[3]http://www.metaquotes.net/

the broker is bad, or because the broker prevented them from losing all their money because of bad trading practices? The latter is more common than you might think.

The bottom line with respect to brokers is you should find one you are comfortable working with and that you trust. Your broker is going to be your best friend during your time as a Forex trader. Spend time with their practice accounts, doing a few trades per day to get a feel for the interface and your potential profits/losses based on your strategy. Do not feel like you need to use the first broker you find; do your research and try a few out. I ended up going back to one of the first brokers I found after trying out about six or seven others. Trust me, the Forex is not going anywhere, and it will be ready for you when you have found your ideal broker.

I want to close out this chapter with a discussion on investors versus traders, since there tends to be some negative bias towards traders. While I talk about trading in this book, I want to make it very clear up front that I consider Forex trading part of a larger investment strategy. In other words trading the Forex is just another tool in the investors toolbox.

2.3 Investor versus Trader

Let us start by looking at the definition of a trader as given by Investopedia[4]:

Trader

> An individual who engages in the transfer of financial assets in any financial market, either for themselves, or on behalf of a someone else.

Now for an investor[5]:

Investor

---

[4]http://www.investopedia.com/terms/t/trader.asp#ixzz1lp7t5O2k
[5]http://www.investopedia.com/terms/i/investor.asp#ixzz1lp8qZ3Db

21

Any person who commits capital with the expectation
of financial returns. Investors utilize investments in
order to grow their money and/or provide an income
during retirement, such as with an annuity.

These definitions line up with the way in which most people would
define an investor and a trader. The most commonly held view is
traders are looking for a quick profit, moving in and out of the markets
as quickly as possible. These are the brazen pirates of the financial
markets looking for loot as quickly as they can find it. Investors on the
other hand like to put their money into longer term financial vehicles
like stocks, bonds, mutual funds, etc, hoping for less risky longer-term
gains.

The main difference between the two, in my opinion, has more to
do with risk than it does with how long you hold on to an investment.
Trading on any market, be it the stock market or the foreign exchange
market, is an investment. Traders will make money or lose money a
lot faster than an investor, but they still invest their money with every
trade. Given the shear size of the Forex, currency traders in particular
are incurring more risk with every trade compared to an investor who
only focuses on something like government backed bonds.

Any type of investment has some risk associated with it. The
more return you want for your investment, the more risk you have to
be willing to take. Traders are often seen as being high risk takers,
and a few lucky ones make a lot of money. Day traders are a great
example of this. A day trader is someone who makes multiple trades
per day, usually on the stock market. A friend of mine was friends
with a stock broker who traded on the TSX. One day he walked in to
work with $1,000, and walked out that afternoon and bought himself
a brand new Porsche[6]! He was the exception, not the rule, and this
was in the early 1990s before the dot-com bubble burst. I'm not sure
he ever repeated that success. The reality is most day traders lose
money in the long run. The risks are too high to make so many trades

---

[6]Roughly $60,000 at the time.

so quickly, since the smallest change could send your entire trading day into chaos. In this book I talk about trading, but I will also show you how to make safe trades to help reduce the risk.

Long term investments that offer little risk help most people sleep at night. Government issued bonds are a great example of this. For example if I bought a series CP15 premium Canada savings bond in 2000 worth $1,000 that matured in 2010 (compounded annually), I would have had an annual interest rate ranging between 2.35 to 5.0% return, giving me a final balance of $1,460.52. So about a 46% return over ten years. Not bad! Low risk since I don't think the government of Canada is going to go bankrupt anytime soon, and a pretty good return overall.

My experience trading the Forex shows a different story though. Using the same $1,000, I could have traded on the Forex and made the same return in less than two years. If the Forex is co-operating and I'm willing to increase my risk, I could easily make that same return in less than a year. Of course I could also lose everything, so it is important to remember to trade within your means and use proper money management techniques that I will be sharing with you in the next few chapters.

Remember the Golden Rule

A good rule of thumb is to never trade more than you are willing to lose. My money tree is made up of a few different types of investments, with Forex being one part of the tree. I do not recommend that anyone put all their investment money into a single type of investment. Spread things around and you will be happier for it in the long run.

So what about me? Well, by definition I am a Forex trader. I hold on to my positions[7] a little longer than some of my more aggressive Forex trader counterparts, usually from a few hours to a few days. When I first started, I was a lot like a stock market day trader, opening and closing my positions a few dozen times a day. I learned the hard way, and quickly realized that there was a lot more for me to learn. I have never forgotten those early lessons, and through some serious trading discipline I have never seen such drastic losses. I still have bad trades; everyone does. I just make sure that my good days more than make up for my bad days.

2.4 Summary

Now that you know what the Forex is, how it compares to other markets like the stock market, who the players are in the Forex as well as what role brokers play. I've given some general guidelines in selecting a broker and I have tried my best to explain the difference between an investor and a trader. Armed with all this newfound knowledge, let us take that first big step on your journey to trading on the Forex. The next chapter will arm you with the tools to overcome one of the biggest hurdles that face most new Forex traders - *terminology*.

---

[7]A position is a way to define how much of a particular currency is held in a particular trade.

Chapter 3

Forex Terminology

Forex has its own terminology that you need to know in order to follow what's going on in the market. There are loads of terms, but you don't need to be familiar with all of them. Some of the terms that you *should* be familiar with are: *pair, pip, ask, bid, spread, interval, candle, order, long, short, lot, triggers, leverage* and *margin call*. I would encourage you to read this chapter a few times if necessary in order to fully understand these terms, or come back here for review. There are quite a few terms to cover, so let's get started.

3.1 Forex Fundamentals

Your first step to learning about Forex is to understand its most basic parts, that is the *Pair, Price* and *Pip*. These will be the core components for the remainder of this book and they will be encountered every time you trade the Forex or even read about it. Thankfully these are also simple concepts, which is also a great way to show how easy Forex trading is to get into.

3.1.1 Pair

When you perform a trade on the Forex market, you are actually either buying or selling a currency. The value of a currency is based on a relationship with another currency, which means that you will see prices given in terms of a *pair* like *EUR/USD*. The *EUR/USD* is the pairing of the euro to the US dollar, giving the world the ability to determine how much one currency is worth by comparing it to the value of another.

As mentioned in Section 2.1, there are some major currencies that are traded on the Forex market. However, since currencies are traded in pairs, there is actually a more common list of currency pairs that traded on the Forex market. Table 3.1 lists these more commonly traded currency pairs that any beginner should consider starting with.

Currency Pair
EUR/USD
EUR/GBP
GBP/USD
USD/CHF
USD/CAD
USD/JPY
AUD/USD
NZD/USD

Table 3.1: Common Forex Currency Pairs

These particular pairs have a trade volume which is fairly high, meaning lots of people trade these currencies actively. A high popularity makes them easier to predict trends for, which translates into profits for people like you and I. Chapter 4 will cover some popular tools used to find (and follow) trends.

Each pair can be broken down into the *Base* and *Quote* currencies. So for EUR/USD, the base currency is the euro and the quote currency is the US dollar. The prices you see are related to the value of the pair in relation to the quote currency. This is complicated somewhat since there are often two prices associated with a currency pair, so let's delve deeper into how Forex prices are provided to traders.

3.1.2 Price

When you look at the price for a currency pair from a broker, you will actually see two prices. This is probably one of the most confusing things to new Forex traders, since the first time you look at it you have no idea what is going on! The two prices you see are called the *Ask* and *Bid* price, and they represent the different prices you pay depending on if you are buying or selling the pair.

The *Ask* price is the amount of the quote currency it will take to buy one unit of the base currency. The *Bid* price is the amount that you can sell one unit of the base currency and get this amount back in the quote currency. Let's take a look at a real example since it will be much clearer.

Let's say that I took a look at my broker and they have posted the following prices for the EUR/USD:

- Ask is 1.30064

- Bid is 1.30031

So the base currency is the euro and the quote currency is the US dollar. Based on the Ask price, it would cost me 1.30064 US dollars to "buy" one euro. Remember that when it comes to the Ask price, the price that is quoted is what it would cost to purchase one unit of the base currency (the euro) using the quote currency (the US dollar). Conversely if I were to "sell" one euro, I would be able to get 1.30031 US dollars for it. This comes from the Bid price.

This is a tricky concept when it comes to Bid/Ask prices, but thankfully you do not have to memorize these rules. Brokers will tell you if you have sufficient funds in your account to make a trade or not. The one thing that you should remember from this is that when you are buying a currency pair, you are buying at the "Ask" price, and when you are selling a currency pair, you are selling at the "Bid" price. Remember that simple rule and you will be set.

So you might be wondering why these prices have so many decimal places. Well, those decimal places are what provide you (the Forex trader) with profit, as well as the fees for your broker. Let's look at *pips* next.

3.1.3   Pip

The term *pip* is actually an acronym for *price interest point*, which as it turns out is really just a measurement for the smallest change that a currency price can make. For most of the pairs given in Table 3.1, a single pip is 0.0001 of the price of that pair. The one exception is for pairs that include the Japanese Yen (JPY), such as USD/JPY. For these pairs, a single pip is 0.01 units.

So how are pips used? Currency prices are measured by their movement in terms of pips, so it's important to know what that means when you are looking at prices. Also, spreads (which are covered in Section 3.1.4) are also measured in terms of pips. Here is a quick example. Right now, at the time of writing this sentence, the Ask price for the EUR/USD is 1.31318 and the Bid price is 1.31307. Waiting a few moments and the Ask price has changed to 1.31284 with the Bid price at 1.31273. This gives a difference of $(1.31318 - 1.31273) \times 10000 = 4.5$ pips.

So how much money does that translate into? It depends on how much you have bought. Let's keep it simple and say that I had bought $e\,10,000$ worth of EUR/USD at 1.31318. The price per pip is then $(0.0001 \div 1.31318) \times 10000 \approx e\,0.76151$ or $0.76151 \times 1.31318 = \$1$ USD[1].

---

[1]For every $10,000$ units of a currency pair that has USD as it's base currency, 1 pip will be equivalent to $1 USD.

Closing the order with a Bid price[2] of 1.31273, the 4.5 pip difference would translate to a loss of $4.50 USD.

You will notice that the prices given above went to 5 decimal places, but earlier I mentioned that pips are normally measured up to 4 decimal places! So what is with this extra decimal point? This extra decimal point is called a *fractional pip* or a *pipette*, not all brokers support pipettes but it is growing in popularity to show how tightly a broker's spreads are. When one broker can say that they offer a pip spread of 1.5 pips for EUR/USD, another might claim that they have a spread of 1.1 pips for EUR/USD!

3.1.4   Spread

We know that the Ask and Bid prices are different and it is this difference that we call the *spread* of the currency pair. Forex brokers do not charge per transaction like most stock brokers do, so then how do they make their money? Through the spread. The spread is measured in pips and it varies from broker-to-broker and even from pair-to-pair. Some brokers offer fixed spreads for their pairs, while others offer flexible spreads that can change. These changes can occur when major announcements are being made (like the current unemployment rate) or when other major events happen that would affect the currency prices.

The Ask price is always going to be higher than the bid price. This is quite literally the opposite of buy low, sell high. Your broker is going to force you to buy at the Ask price (the high) and sell at the Bid price (the low). Brokers want you to hold on to positions for a while, and the spread helps them give you incentive to do so.

---

[2]When you close an order you do the opposite of what opened that order, so a buy order gets closed out at the sell price. Section 3.3.1 will help explain this further.

Scalping

There is a technique that some Forex traders do called *scalping*, which is where you buy and sell currencies rapidly, with as little as 0.1 pips profit. You don't make a lot with each trade, but you make up for that with the high number of trades. It's a lot like fast food chains. Their profit margins are really small, but they make up for it in volume. Don't be a scalper. Most reputable brokers will quit you as a client if you are caught scalping. With the right techniques, it's easy to make a few pips of profit per trade.

The basic rule of thumb is that the smaller the spread, the better for you. Fixed spreads make it easier to know exactly what you stand to make or lose, regardless of any critical news events, but they often come at a price of higher spreads or brokers requiring that you have a large account balance. Critical market events are predictable, usually only a few times per month depending on the currencies you are trading. Variable spreads for these events generally only last a few hours, so unless you plan on trading during those periods, it may not be worth moving to a fixed spread. There is no right or wrong answer here; it really does boil down to what you are comfortable with.

3.2 Charting Terms

Section 3.1 covered the basic topics that you need to know in order to understand how to read a Forex price and how the Bid and Ask price are related to one another.

This was a great start, but there are a few more concepts you need to learn before you can read a Forex *chart*. In this section we will cover the terms and concepts related to charts you will encounter in your Forex trading career. There are a lot of different charts available to Forex traders, but I will be focusing on the *candlestick* charts specifically for the rest of this book.

What is a candlestick chart? I suppose it might be a good idea to start with what a candle is and work our way from there.

3.2.1 Candle

A *candle* is at the heart of a candlestick chart. So what exactly is a candle? A candle is basically a rectangular box that may have a stick (called a wick) at the top and bottom of it. It is used to show the open, high, low and close price for a particular interval. Figure 3.1 gives an example of the two types of candle you would see on a candlestick chart.

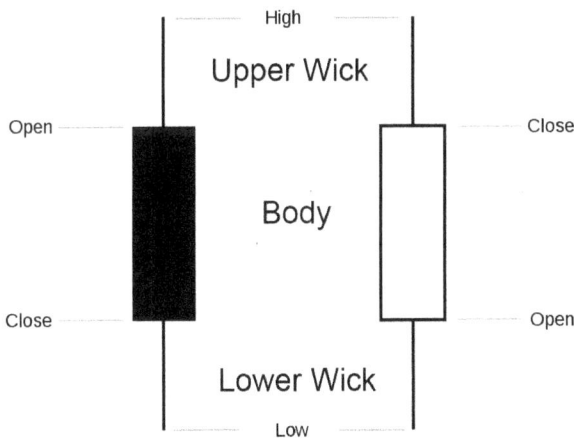

Figure 3.1: The basic candle types used in a candlestick chart

The main difference between the two candles is the body. If the body is *empty* (like the candle on the right), then that means the open price was lower than the close price for that interval. In other words, the price for the currency pair is going up. If the candle has a *filled-in or colored* body, then that means the opening price is higher than the closing price for that interval. In other words, the price of the currency pair is going down.

The wicks on either end of the candle are the high and low points for the price during that period. Not all candles will have wicks, which means that the open or close price was the highest or lowest point for that candle.

The one take-away from this section is knowing what the two different candle types are. An empty candle indicates upward price movement while a shaded candle represents a downward price movement.

Since a candle represents a single interval, you can see the open and close indicators of what the currency pair was worth at the beginning and the end of that interval[3], respectively. For example if we were looking at a 15 minute chart and I look at the candle for 14:30, then the open price is the value of the pair at 14:15 and the close price is the value of the pair at 14:30, with the high and low wicks representing the highest and lowest prices during that time period respectively.

The Cult Of The Candlestick

Candlestick charts are incredibly popular amongst Forex traders, commodity traders, stock traders, etc. Naturally with such popularity you will get all sorts of theories about how to properly trade them. The candlestick charts that I provide here are the basic, run-of-the-mill *Open, High, Low, Close (OHLC)* candlesticks. There is another variety of candles known as *Heikin-Ashi* candles,

---

[3]Intervals will be covered in Section 3.2.2.

which use a modified calculation for the open, high, low and close prices. Take a look at them if you would like, but I have had mixed results with them. To keep things simple, I would stick with these standard candlesticks and explore Heikin-Ashi when you are more comfortable.

Different candlesticks aren't the only thing that people have come up with. There are **a lot** of patterns that people have come up with over the years to identify different candlestick formations that are signals of events to come. Things like *doji star*, *hammer*, *engulfing*, *piercing*, ...and the list goes on. Yes, these are the real names of some common candlestick patterns!

Some traders swear by these patterns. There are a mountain of books available on the subject, and most Forex books include at least a chapter on them. My personal experience is that they are difficult to spot on most charts for new traders. I also found that you would get two conflicting patterns in the same chart, which of course would lead to confusion, frustration, and mistakes when making a trade.

I am not a fan of using candlestick formations when trading Forex, especially for a beginner. There is a lot of fascinating reading available if you are interested. However just like with Heikin-Ashi candles, I would recommend you wait until you are comfortable with trading Forex before you branch out. There is an awful lot of patterns, and they are not always easy to spot. The rest of this book will cover what I believe are an easier set of tools to get started. Chapter 4 and chapter 5 will cover these more "new trader"-friendly tools.

A *candlestick chart* is just a collection of candles over a specific time period or *interval*. Before I give an example of what a candlestick chart looks like, it might be a good idea to discuss *intervals*, since you will be working with them when you are looking at a chart.

33

3.2.2 Interval

An *interval* is a way of looking at a currency pair's activity over a given time range at regular points in time. For example, I may want to look at the prices for USD/JPY from January 1, 2012 through to February 1, 2012 at a 4 hour interval. Figure 3.2 gives an example of what this chart would look like.

As you can see, each candle represents a 4-hour block of time, with the open price being the beginning of that 4-hour period, the close being the end of that 4-hour period and the high and low values spanning the maximum and minimum price that fall within that time period.

What time periods are available for viewing often depends on what your charting software has available. Table 3.2 lists some of the most popular time periods used by Forex traders and the acronyms often associated with them.

Interval	Acronym
1 Minute	M1
5 Minutes	M5
15 Minutes	M15
30 Minutes	M30
1 Hour	H1
4 Hours	H4
1 Day	D1
1 Week	W1
Monthly	MN

Table 3.2: Common Chart Intervals

Depending on the charting software you are using, your interval selection may be different. When you are first starting out I would suggest that you stick with the *H4* chart simply because it is one of the easiest charts to get trends for. The downside is that your first

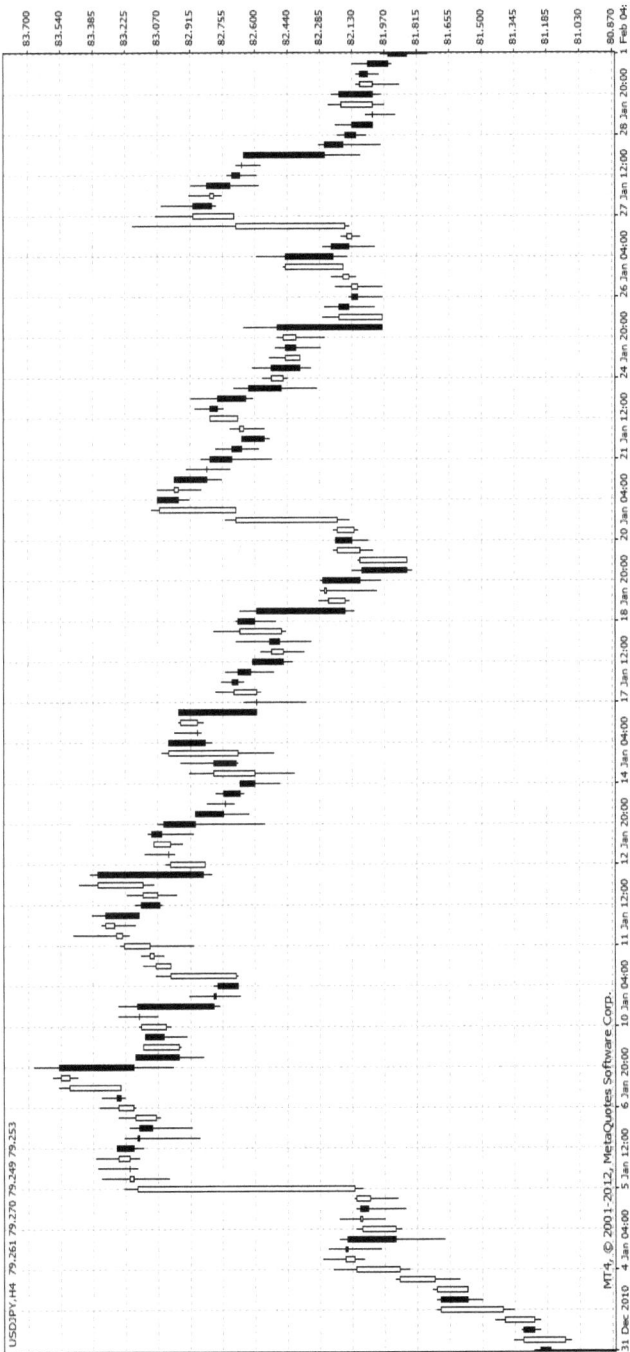

Figure 3.2: USD/JPY - 4 Hour Chart - January 1, 2012 - February 1, 2012

few trades are going to take a while to potentially make you some money. I definitely would not recommend going lower than the *H1* chart, simply because at 15- and 30-minutes, the charts can get very volatile very quickly. Volatility means that new traders end up losing a lot more than they bargained for, especially if they are not prepared for that volatility.

Once you get more experienced and comfortable with trading one time period, you may want to start exploring other time periods. A common technique more experienced traders use is that they look at a long period chart like H4, then look at charts like M30 or even M15 for entry points to maximize their profits. Again this comes with experience, so do make sure you fully understand trends and trend movements before you try to do this.

3.3 Orders, Lots and Triggers - Oh My!

Let's have a quick recap. You should understand the basic terms and concepts a Forex trader needs to know, you know how to read a candlestick chart and what different intervals mean. It's time for the last part of your terminology training, namely understanding the terms and concepts related to making actual Forex trades. This section will cover leverage, orders, lots, triggers and margin calls. All of these are the final pieces in your initiation into Forex trading.

3.3.1 Order

As we saw in Section 3.1.2, you buy and sell currency pairs at different prices. So when you buy something like USD/CHF, you are buying US dollars using Swiss francs. So you can either buy or sell a currency pair, those are the basic options when we talk about types of orders. Of course being a Forex trader means that you get to call these order types something far more interesting - *Long* or *Short* orders.

A *Long* order (or going long on a given pair) is when you decide to place a buy order, purchasing the base currency with the quote currency at the Ask price. Similarly when you want to sell a currency pair, you are placing a *Short* order (or *shorting* a given pair) by selling the base currency for the Bid price of the quote currency. These terms can be confusing at first, but I suggest you get used to them since they are used in pretty much any trading environment including stocks, commodities and futures.

What Are You Buying And Selling?

When you buy a pair, or place a *Long* order, you are buying the base currency using the quote currency. So if I place a Long order for USD/JPY, I am using Japanese Yen to buy more US dollars. Assuming the price went up, when I close the order I sell those US dollars at a higher exchange rate for the Japanese Yen allowing me to end up with more Yen than when I started. Profit!

The opposite is true when you sell a pair, or place a *Short* order. That is, you are selling the base currency and buying the quote currency. Again in the case of USD/JPY, if I place a Short order then I am selling US dollars and buying Japanese Yen. Assuming the price did indeed drop, when I close this type of order I buy back more US dollars than I started with because the Japanese Yen is worth more due to the falling price of US dollars! Again, profit!

This is one of the most confusing concepts for new traders when they are buying and selling currencies. Don't get hung up on these details, just understand that when trading Forex both "buy low, sell high!" **and** "sell high, buy low!" apply!

The old stock trader's adage of *buy low, sell high* applies to Forex as well - it just so happens that you can also sell high and buy low!

This is a neat concept since you have the opportunity to earn money regardless of the direction the price goes. Trading Forex is a lot different than trading stocks since with stocks you generally are looking for an opportunity to buy in at a low price and sell at a higher price[4]. Forex gives you a lot more opportunities, and since the market is so huge, there is always someone to take you up on your offer.

Who Are You Trading With?

In the stock market, you cannot buy or sell shares unless there is someone on the other side who is willing to sell or buy from you respectively. The same is true when you trade the Forex. The biggest difference is that while you may not be able to find a willing partner in your stock trade, you will virtually never run into this situation when you trade the Forex. Because the Forex market is so large, there is almost always someone willing to take your trade, either long or short.

Some people believe that this makes the Forex market somehow "unfair" to traders, since someone is always going to be on the losing side. Not necessarily, since the other party might be trading different time frames, watching a longer trend, etc. There is a lot more complexity to the relationship between Forex traders than most people realize. For a new Forex trader, it is sufficient to know that you won't have to worry about not finding someone who is willing to help fill your order.

Orders do come in a variety of different flavors, names and options. Check with your broker to see what different names they have and the

---

[4]I understand that you can also issue short orders with stocks, but this is generally not for the newcomer and can be considered a more risky venture for new stock market traders. Forex is a little more flexible in this regard.

different options for placing orders. Two of the most common order types are the *Market Order* and the *Limit Order*.

- A *Market Order* is an order that is filled at the current price. That is the Ask price if you are going long, or the Bid price if you are shorting the pair.

- A *Limit Order* is an order that will only be filled if the pair's price reaches a pre-determined value.

Most new traders will be making market orders. Limit orders are usually used by people who are trying to predict a trend and want to get in on the trend as early as possible. The one important thing to remember about limit orders is that they **do not** guarantee you will place your order at the price you set your limit at, but rather your order will be placed shortly thereafter. Depending on any delays between your broker and the wider Forex market, your order may be filled at a different price. If you do decide to use limit orders, just be aware of this possibility.

One last aspect of orders is how large each order should be. Different brokers allow you to define an order size differently. Some brokers allow you to specify individual *units* when placing an order. For example, one unit in a Long order for the USD/CAD would be equivalent to buying one US dollar at the Ask price using the Canadian dollar whereas one unit in a short order would be selling one US dollar to receive the Bid price in Canadian dollars.

However, most brokers use *lots*, which is a standardized order size. Let's look at lots next.

3.3.2 Lots

A *standard lot* is $100,000$ units of a given currency. For a long order, it is $100,000$ units of the base currency. Some brokers also let you trade a *mini lot* which is $10,000$ units, or even a *micro lot*, which is $1,000$ units. If we were trading the GBP/USD and created a long order for one standard lot, then I would be buying £$100,000$ at the

Ask price. A mini lot would be £10,000, and a micro lot would be £1,000.

Some brokers do not trade in lots, but instead allow you to place orders using individual *units*. A *unit* is a single denomination of a currency, such as 1 US dollar or 1 Japanese yen. This is less common, and is debatable if it is better or worse than using lots. Lots make it easier to do calculations in your head regarding how much money you are risking with each trade, but being able to tailor orders right down to a single unit offers a lot more flexibility in terms of risk management. My personal preference is to use individual units, but that is mainly because I like the compounding effect I can achieve using individual units.

3.3.3 Triggers

A *trigger* is a pre-determined price level that will cause some type of action.

There are two main types of triggers, the *stop loss (SL)* trigger and the *take profit (TP)* trigger:

- A *Stop Loss (SL)* trigger is a target price where you want to automatically close your order so you can limit your losses.

- A *Take Profit (TP)* trigger is a target price where you want to automatically close your order so you can realize some pre-determined amount of profit.

In this book, I will provide SL and TP levels in terms of pips from the price an order was placed at, but your broker may offer the ability to define these triggers differently, such as a certain percentage of loss/gain. The end result is the same but the semantics in getting there may be slightly different.

One important thing to note is that these triggers are a lot like limit orders. Just because they are set does not necessarily mean that they will be hit at those exact levels. A lot of this depends on how volatile the market is when one of these triggers is hit. The less volatile the market, the more likely the triggers will close at the price you set them at.

Using Triggers

I only have one recommendation in regards to using triggers:

> # ALWAYS SET A STOP LOSS TRIGGER WITH EVERY TRADE!

Not everyone sets a SL trigger when they create their orders. These are usually the same people who lose all their money and then complain about how the market has some sort of personal vendetta against them. Don't be foolish; always, **ALWAYS** set a SL with any order order you place. It is your best insurance policy to make sure that you do not empty out your account balance because of a bad trade[5].

The use of a TP is another story completely. As with SL triggers, not everyone sets a TP trigger. I think it's nice to know how much money you could be making on a trade, so it certainly doesn't hurt to set a TP trigger when you create an order. Some people's reason for not setting a TP trigger is because they want to have greater control of their order. They argue that they will "just know" when it's time to close out an order. They also like to watch price charts for hours on end, sweating over every pip. Personally I like to have a life outside of my trades, so I generally always set a TP to ensure that I'll get some type of profit should the market go my way.

---

[5]Actually your broker will close your order for you automatically if it loses too much money - see Section 3.3.5

Sometimes when you set a TP, the market will hit your trigger and continue to move past it. This means you could have made more money if you had only kept the order open a little longer! Why oh why did you set that TP trigger! This is another one of the excuses people give when they explain why they do not set a TP when they place an order.

Let me tell you a secret - beginners rarely know when to get out! In Chapter 4 I go over some tools to help you identify when a trend may be reversing, but being able to use these tools effectively takes a lot of practice. Trying to use them right away without having a TP trigger in place is like reading a book about lions and then going on a hunting safari in Africa! Book knowledge alone doesn't translate well, you need to practice first. Look at it another way, would you rather know ahead of time how much you could safely make or would you like to gamble with each trade you place? Knowing your potential returns can help ease your nerves in the long run.

What do successful traders do?

This actually leads to an important point. Did you know that most successful traders only hit their TP levels about 20% to 45% of the time? The rest of the time is spent either closing out at a loss when their SL is hit or because the market trend has reversed and they switch positions. So how exactly do they make any money, let alone a living? Simple, it's all about the ratio.

You will often hear about a risk:reward ratio for a trade. The ratio

SL:TP is the risk:reward ratio, where the general rule of thumb is the lower this ratio is, the better for your order. If the SL is higher than the TP, then you have a problem since that means you are risking more pips than you are willing to make. To play it safe, you never want to risk losing more pips than you are willing to make. Many first time traders ignore this, and I was no exception. But that is a story for another chapter.

So at the very least what you want is a risk:reward ratio of 1:1. In reality it's a better idea to have a risk:reward ratio of 1 : 3 or even 1 : 4. What this means is that you are willing to risk 1 pip of loss in the hopes of making 3 - 4 pips of profit. Depending on how big your order is, that could be a pretty hefty profit! To look at it another way, you only need to be right 20% of the time if your risk:reward ratio was 1:4 in order to break even. Anything more than that is pure profit. "Successful" traders are only successful about 40 - 60% of the time. So how exactly do they make money? They ensure that their risk:reward ratio is better than 1:1, usually opting for 1:4 or a higher reward value.

Now finding an appropriate SL and TP trigger level is tricky; if it were easy everyone would be rich! Suffice it to say that there are a few different ways to do this, and there really is no "perfect" way to figure out the right levels. Some tools of the trade including trend lines, Fibonacci Retracements, MFE/MAE analysis, etc. I would recommend using a fixed pip-size for the SL and TP triggers. It will be easier to understand and since you can already know the risks involved it can make focusing on the other tools that much easier. I'll give an example of this strategy in Chapter 6 when I walk you through a full month of trading.

Next up I want to cover the double edge sword that can both give unbelievable reward as well as create unbelievable losses - leverage.

3.3.4 Leverage

Leverage is not unique to Forex, but if you have never heard of it before it can be a pretty cool concept. Leverage allows you to "borrow" money from your broker in order to open orders and make trades. This is why you see brokers saying that you can open up an account with them for as little as $100 USD.

Leverage is usually expressed as a ratio, like 20:1, 50:1 or even 100:1. For example, if I use a 50:1 leverage and I had $1,000 USD in my account, I would have $50,000[6] USD available to trade with!

Leverage is a wonderful tool, but it does have a set of requirements that go along with it. Brokers require that you maintain a certain percentage of funds in your account to cover the funds that you are "leveraging" from them. This percentage is known as the *minimum required margin*. The minimum required margin depends on the leverage ratio you are trading with. Table 3.3 gives a list of common leverage ratios and their associated minimum required margin percentages.

These minimum margin requirements are rules that your broker uses to ensure that you have enough funds to cover opening a new trade. The money you put in your account is used as collateral by your broker when you use their funds to leverage your own.

However it's not all sunshine and flowers. If you have an open

---

[6]($1,000 \times 50$)

Leverage	Minimum Margin %
100:1	1%
50:1	2%
30:1	3.3%
20:1	5%
10:1	10%

Table 3.3: Leverage Ratios

order that is running an unrealized[7] loss and you do not have enough funds in your account to cover this loss, you risk facing the dreaded *margin call*. Let's explore that next.

3.3.5   Margin Call

A *Margin Call* is broker's demand to add more funds to your account in order to cover any outstanding debt you face due to an open order/trade. Essentially if you have an open trade, and that trade goes in the wrong direction and you quickly approach a point where you do not have sufficient funds in your account to cover these losses, your broker may issue a *margin call*.

Not all brokers are created equal - some brokers will simply close your order(s) if there are insufficient funds in your account to cover the losses. Other brokers will let you know that a margin call is pending and give you time to either add more funds to your account or let you ride out the risk. Of course if you reach near zero, then all brokers will happily close your orders and potentially wipe out your account.

---

[7]Any trade that has not yet closed and any potential profit/loss associated with that open trade is considered *unrealized*.

Some less reputable brokers may even let you run into the red with them, potentially owing them more money than you started with.

Most regulation agencies will protect you from that happening though, which is another reason why you want to go with a broker that is registered with some regulatory agency in the country from where they operate. The point is that no broker will let you get to the point where you owe them more money than what you have in your account. Nearly every legitimate broker I know will never let you reach a point where you owe them money, but they will all happily let you run your account down to zero.

So what should you take away from all of this? First off, don't be fooled into thinking that a higher leverage is better. You definitely have the ability to make a lot of money with very little invested, but most Forex brokers will close your orders with a margin call before you get the chance to "strike it rich". This is mainly due to the fact that the brokers themselves don't want to lose any money, hence the reason why they have these rules in place.

In 2009, the United States updated the rules for regulated US Forex firms that capped their maximum leverages to 100:1 for the major currency pairs and 25:1 for the rest. I was actually with a broker that offered up to a 200:1 ratio, and they actively encouraged their customers to switch to another one of their divisions which was based in Europe so that they could continue to use this higher leverage! I promptly left that broker since it was clear to me that they were more intent on preying on the inexperienced rather than help them become better traders.

My current broker has a maximum leverage of 50:1, but I generally trade with a 20:1 leverage. When you're just starting out on your own using manual trading techniques, I would start with at least a 10:1 leverage but not more than a 20:1 leverage. You may not make as much money on each trade, but you won't lose as much either if/when you make a mistake.

3.4 Summary

Whew! This was a long chapter covering a lot of terminology and concepts. I strongly recommend that you re-read this chapter a few times until you are comfortable with all these terms and concepts before moving on. Not only will it save you a lot of confusion, it will make for a much smoother trading experience overall.

Of course terms and concepts alone won't help you know when you should open that first order or when you should close out an order before it hits your SL trigger. The next chapter will help prepare you for that journey by introducing you to some of the basic tools you can use to make money trading currencies on the Forex. *Trend indicators* are the tools to help you find market trends, which can help you know when to go long or short.

CHAPTER 4

Trends Aren't Just For Hipsters

How do you know when to buy (go *Long*) or sell (go *Short*)? Guessing only goes so far, and it won't work long term. So what do you do? Like most things in life, having the right tools will help make this a lot less stressful and a lot more profitable. The right tools help you get the job done quickly, correctly and most importantly, safely. *Technical indicators* are tools traders use to make successful trades.

So what exactly *is* a technical indicator? Technical indicators are mathematical tools and models used in technical analysis to give you some indication for the direction the price is going for a given currency pair. Put another way, technical indicators are used by traders to figure out if they should buy or sell a currency pair. That's it. *Technical analysis* is just a fancy way of telling someone the type of tools you use when you trade Forex.

I know what you're thinking. *Math?! Really? I don't want to deal with crazy amounts of math!* In all honesty you don't need to. All the tools that I cover are available in any decent trading software system, so aside from providing a parameter or two for the indicator (which often already has a default value) there is no need to fully understand the mathematics behind them[1].

When a trader uses technical indicators for execution of the majority of their trades, they are considered *technical traders*. The others are *fundamental traders*.

Fundamental Traders

Fundamental traders will trade on, well, fundamentals. Calling them traders who trade the news isn't exactly right, but it isn't completely wrong either. Fundamental traders will keep track of things like GDP, unemployment, non-farm payroll, manufacturing and other similar types of reports that would affect a currency's price and trade accordingly. Often times expectations are made that will influence the markets, and when the actual report comes out, it will continue to influence the market. I will not cover fundamental trading any further in this book, but I would encourage you to look into this type of trading later. At the very least learning a bit about fundamental trading may help you decipher what the business reporter is talking about when you watch the news.

But enough about that; I want to show you how some simple

---

[1] If you are interested in the math, grab a copy of *New Concepts in Technical Trading Systems* by J. Welles Wilder.

technical indicators work and how to get those tools to start making some money for you on the Forex[2]. Let's start with the simplest indicator, the *trend line*.

4.1 Trend Lines

When trading the Forex it is important to know what direction the market is moving in. Is it going up or down? The direction the market is going in is called the *trend*. A *trend line* is literally what it sounds like - it is a line that follows the trend. Trend lines are the first tool that most new Forex traders learn about because they are very, very simple. If you can draw a straight line, then you can use a trend line. When I was first learning Forex trading, many of the books I was reading showed examples of how well a trend line would fit the chart they were looking at. I would see examples like the one in Figure 4.1.

Unfortunately when I went to draw my own trend lines, I would encounter charts like the one in Figure 4.2.

So where was the disconnect? Why could I never find a way to draw a trend line like the ones I was seeing in my books? It turns out that I was not paying attention to the charts and I didn't realize how volatile those charts were. A trend line can be drawn on pretty much any chart, it's just a question of understanding *how* to do it. Let's start there and get a better understanding on how to draw a trend line.

---

[2]The information I provide in this book is just a small taste of the different tools that technical traders use. In this chapter I will focus on the tools that *I* have found most useful when I first began my Forex journey.

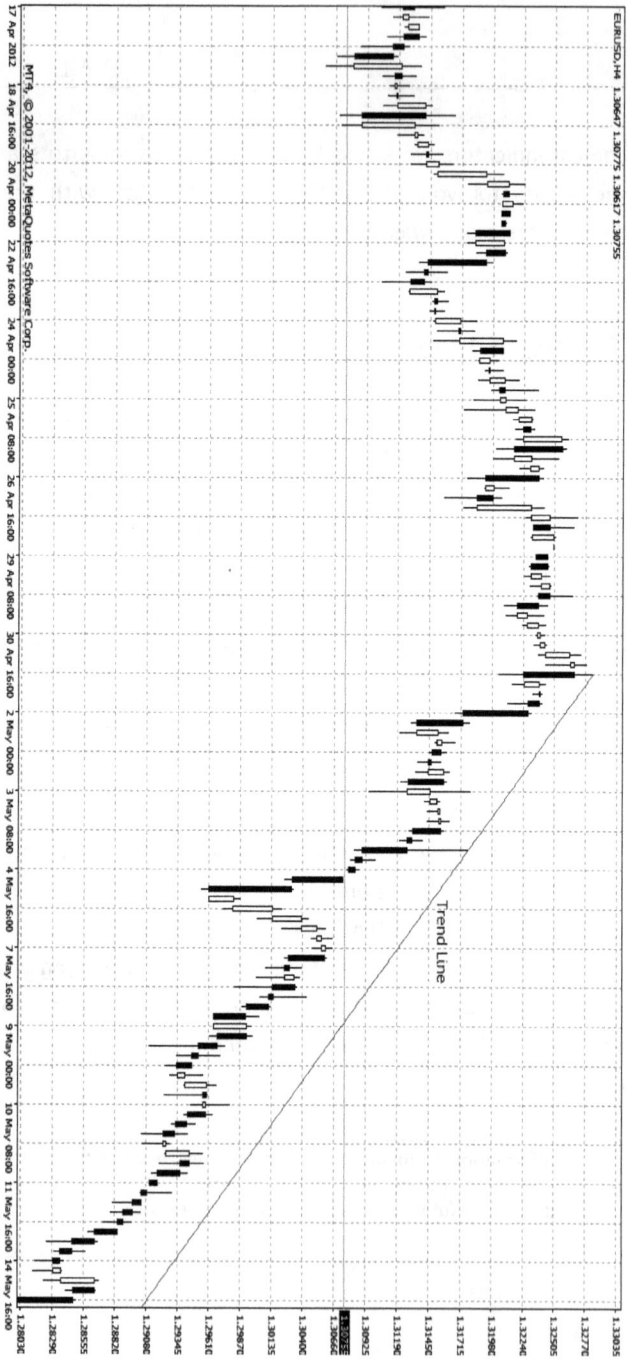

Figure 4.1: An Ideal Trend Line

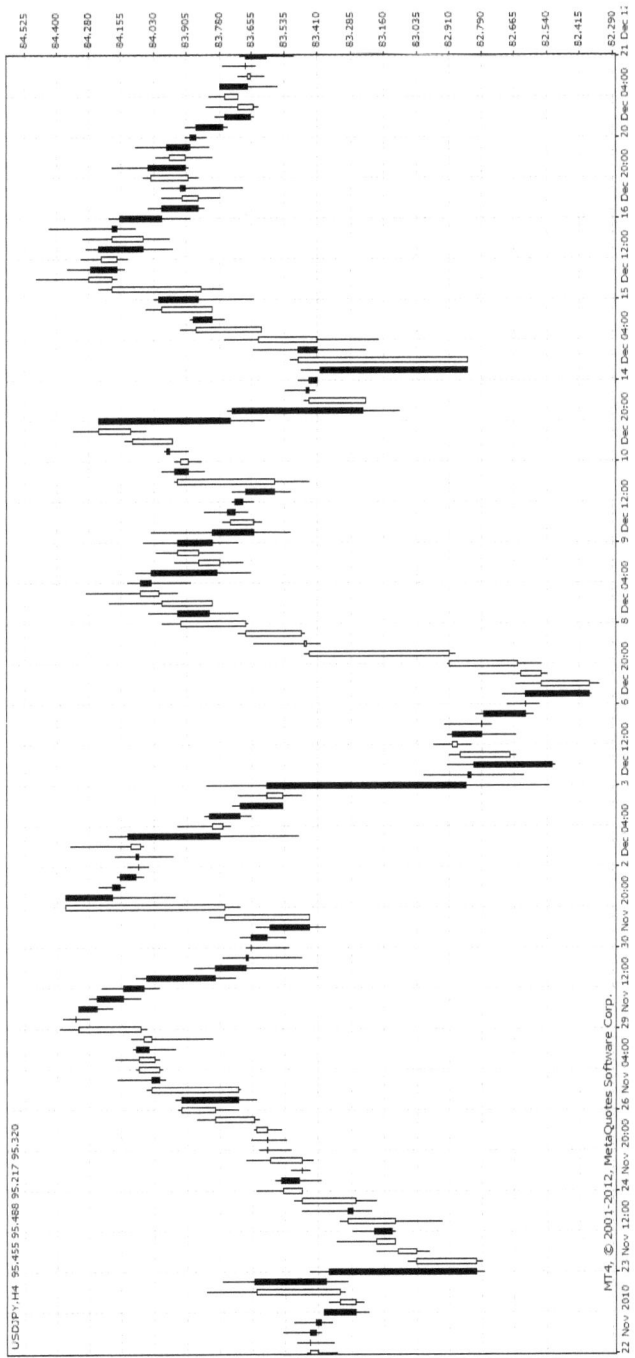

Figure 4.2: A Common Chart - How Can I Put A Trend Line On This?!

4.1.1 Drawing Trend Lines

Trend lines can help you identify if the market is going up or going down for a particular currency pair. Figure 4.3 shows how an uptrend line is drawn.

Notice how during an uptrend we draw the line so it connects only at the bottoms of the candles? That is the first thing you need to know about drawing an upward trend line, the line must start at the low wick of one candle and end at the low wick of another candle. Another way to remember this is to think of an uptrend as being supported from below, as if the market is lifting the prices higher and higher. This is why you see this type of trend line often referred to as a *support trend line* or a *level of support*.

When you draw an upwards trend line, pick a starting candle that is lower than the others and an ending candle that is higher than the starting candle. Use your charting software to draw a line connecting the end of the low wick of the starting candle all the way to the top of the upper wick of the ending candle. If there are some candles that dip below the line but the overall trend continues upwards, that's fine. This is often the first mistake newcomers make when they try to draw a trend line. It's very rare every single candle will fit properly on any type of trend line, and it definitely is not a requirement.

When Trend Lines Are Broken

There will be times when candles break through the support line. Depending on the severity of the break, this may indicate the

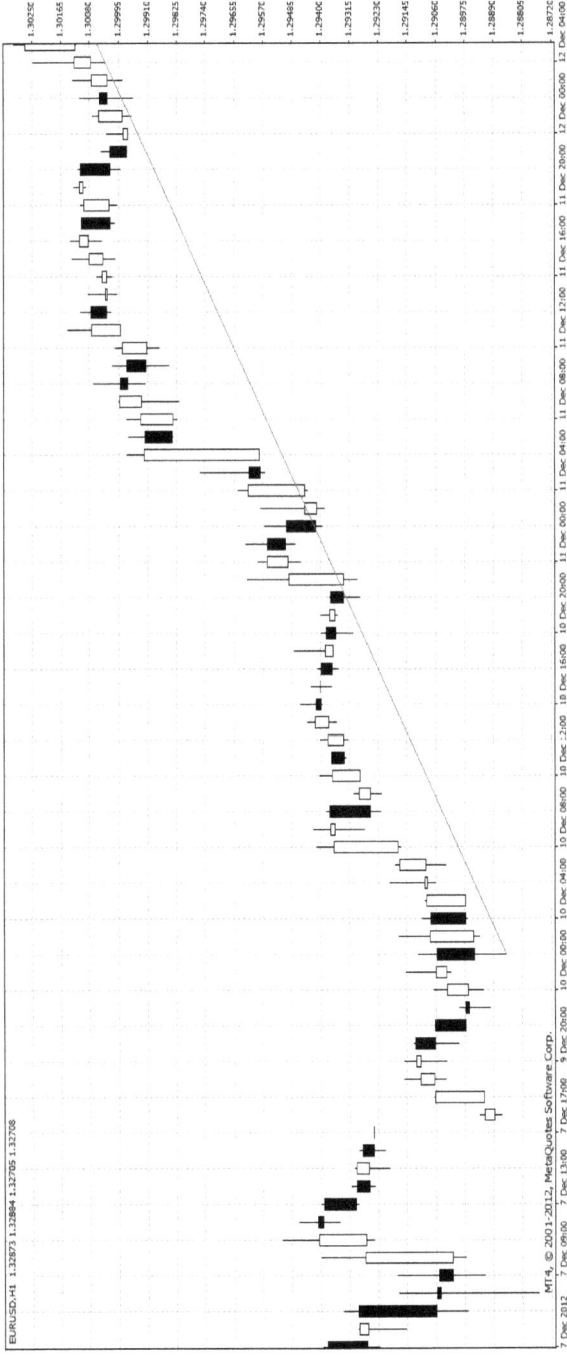

Figure 4.3: Upwards Trend/Level of Support

market is reversing and you should sell. Unfortunately it isn't as simple as that. You will want to get confirmation from other indicators this is indeed the case, but I'll go over that in a later chapter.

So what about a downtrend? Figure 4.4 shows how a downtrend line is drawn.

Downward trend lines are drawn connecting high wick to high wick, which is the exact opposite of the upward trend line. This type of trend line is sometimes called the *level of resistance*, since it seems to exert a type of downwards pressure on the price.

4.1.2 Interpreting Trend Lines

Great, so now you know when you should jump into a trade, right? I mean, if you buy or sell when the price crosses either the level of support or level of resistance you know the price is reversing and so you can jump in and make our fortune, right? Right?! If only it were that easy.

Drawing trend lines may be one of the most frustrating things a new trader will ever face. Why? On the surface it would seem the opposite would be true. Indeed, I have known traders who have used a simple ruler held up to their monitor to make a trend line since it was faster than using the drawing tool. So, if it's so simple a ruler is all you need, why are they hard?

Very often, trend lines are hard to spot in a market that is all over the place. Figure 4.2 is actually a more common pattern in most

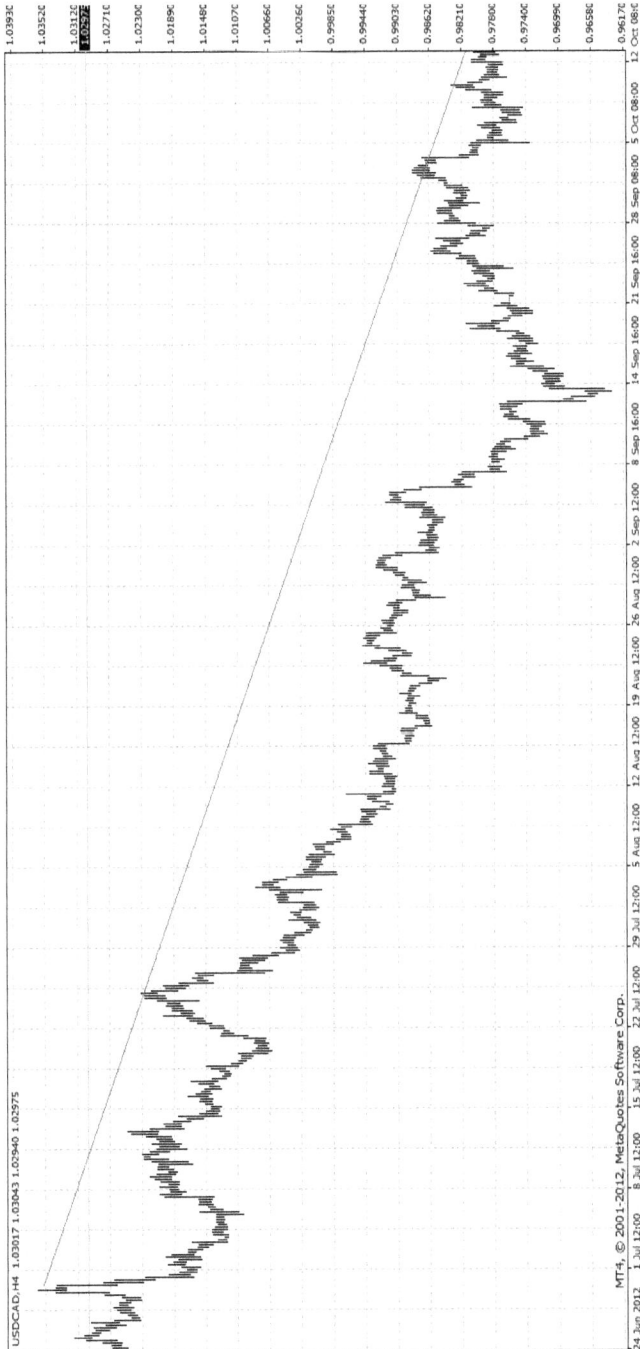

Figure 4.4: Downwards Trend/Level of Resistance

currency charts, so trying to find a good place to draw a trend line can be tricky. It will take practice and patience.

Here is a little secret about trend lines, *trend lines work best for long term trends, not short term trends.* There, now you know. Trend lines are good at giving you an idea of the long term potential for a currency pair's price, but they are better suited for longer time period charts. What constitutes longer time period charts? At the very minimum a 1 hour (H1) chart should be used, but the 4 hour (H4) or even 1 day (D1) charts would be advisable.

One strength of trend lines is to identify when the market is changing direction. For example, Figure 4.5 shows the price breaking through the resistance trend line and it begins to pick up steam. However simply seeing a break-out is not enough. Is it a real break-out, or is the market trying to fake you out and will actually continue the trend?

As we can see in Figure 4.6, the chart showed a break through the line of resistance, but after a short time it continued to follow the original trend. This is why you cannot trust a single indicator when you make your decisions on when to get in or out of a trade.

There are an awful lot of technical indicators available, with trend lines being one of the simplest. As we have seen, however, being a simple indicator doesn't mean that it is easy or even reliable in all cases. I consider trend lines to be a type of early warning system, but I personally don't use them much in my day to day trading. Instead, I like something a little more flexible to help identify trends - *moving averages.*

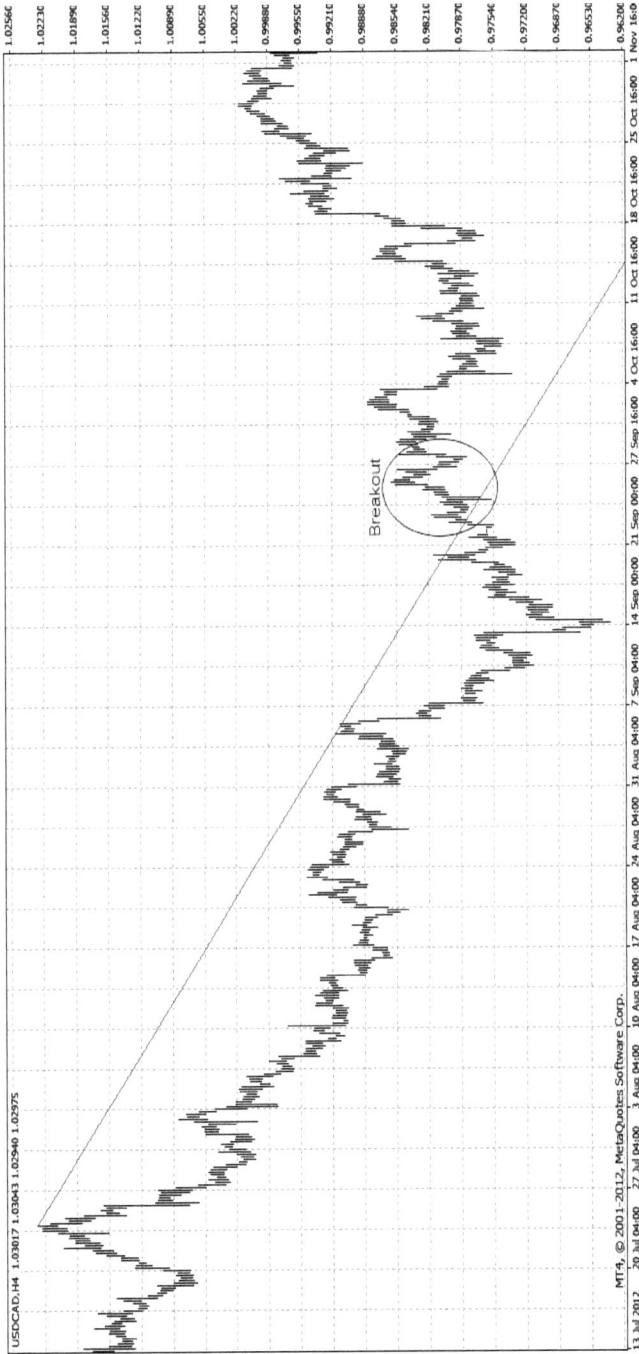

Figure 4.5: Example of a Break-out

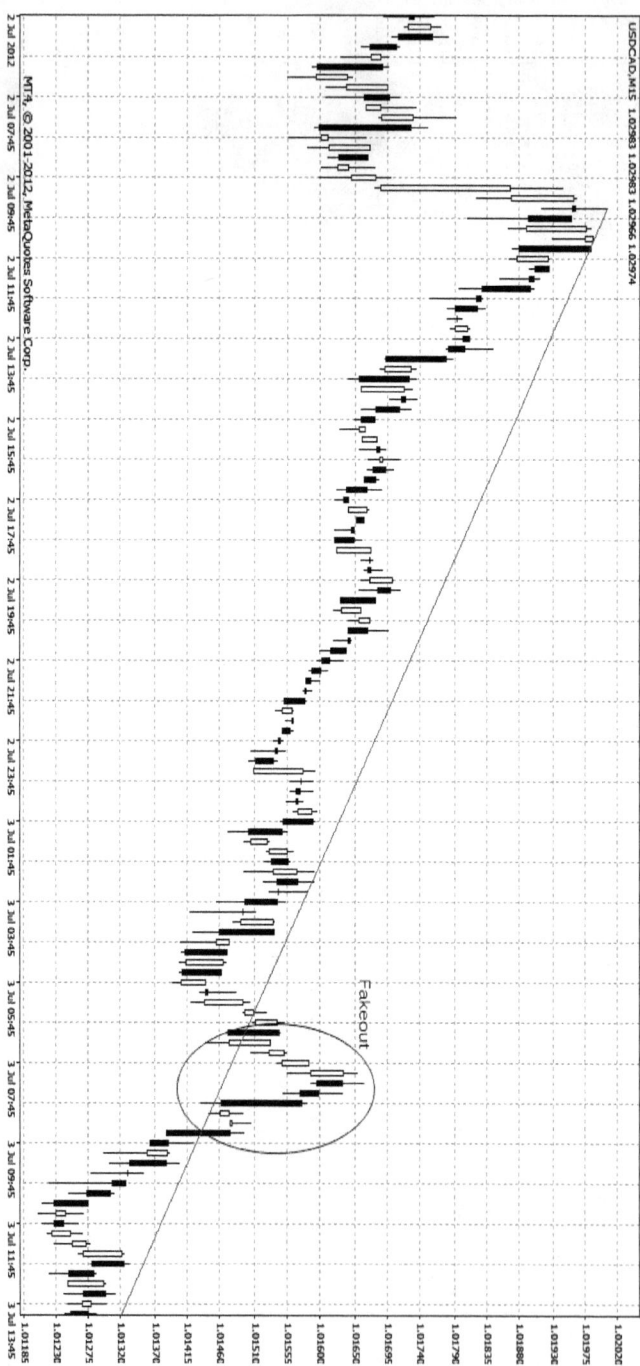

Figure 4.6: Example of a Fake-out

4.2 Moving Averages

Moving averages are one of the most popular tools in the toolbox of the technical trader, and for good reason. They are very flexible, work well to identify trends, and are fairly simple to understand.

A moving average is a way to look at the close price of a currency pair over a certain time period, plotting out how it compares to previous values. The count of the number of prices used is referred to as the *period* of the moving average. You can consider the period to be a sliding window over the price range, where only the most recent close prices are visible. So, if I use a moving average with a period size of 25, the last 25 close prices for the pair are used to calculate the value of the moving average.

There are quite a few different moving averages such as the *simple moving average*, *exponential moving average*, *weighted moving average*, *double exponential moving average*, and so on. I will focus on the first two, as they are the most commonly encountered.

4.2.1 Simple Moving Average

The *Simple Moving Average (SMA)* is just an average of the close prices over the specified number of periods. That is, it sums all the close prices for the specified period and divides this sum by the size of the period. Mathematics types would call this the *arithmetic mean*, but a simple average is just fine. Figure 4.7 gives an example of what a SMA looks like when it is plotted on a chart.

While the SMA is easy to use and understand, it does have a weakness. Since it does not treat any of the close prices any differently, if you have one extreme price in your period data, it may skew the re-

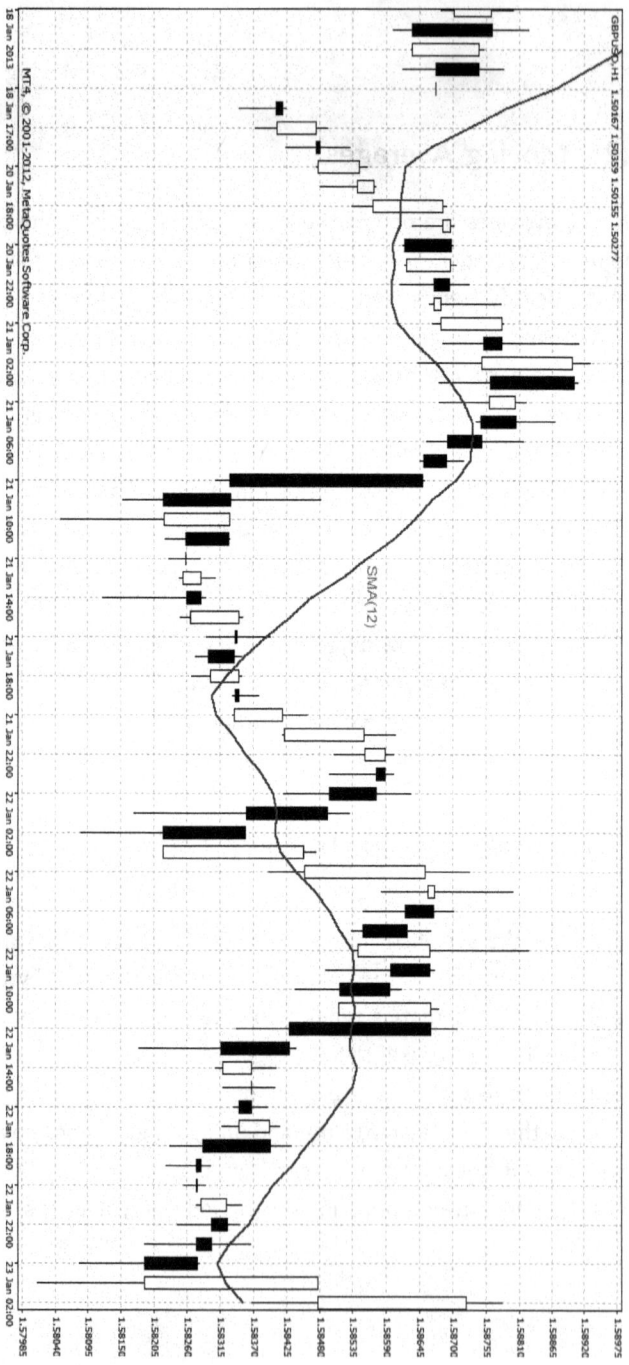

Figure 4.7: Example of a SMA(12) Indicator

sulting SMA calculation. As a result, the *exponential moving average* was born.

4.2.2 Exponential Moving Average

The *Exponential Moving Average* (*EMA* for short) is another popular choice amongst Forex traders for a moving average. It differs from the SMA in that it "ages" the older close prices, making it more responsive to sudden price changes. The calculation is somewhat more complex compared to the SMA, but you honestly don't need to know the math behind it as every charting system I have ever used provides both the EMA and SMA, so you don't need to know how they are calculated. Figure 4.8 is an example of an EMA being plotted on a chart.

As you can see, the EMA plots the price a bit better in terms of the overall trend because it puts more emphasis on the more recent close prices when calculating the moving average. Because of this, the EMA is the preferred moving average to use for "small" periods[3]. So how do they differ? Figure 4.9 show their relationship.

As you can see, the EMA tends to stick closer to the actual candles than the SMA does. Now that you have a basic understanding of how the SMA and EMA work, let's dive right in and see how we can use these moving averages to identify trends - and hopefully make some money out of them.

4.2.3 How To Use Moving Averages

The most basic way to use moving averages is to plot two of them at different time periods and look for a *crossover*. A crossover is when

---

[3]I interpret "small" to be anything less than 12 - 14 periods.

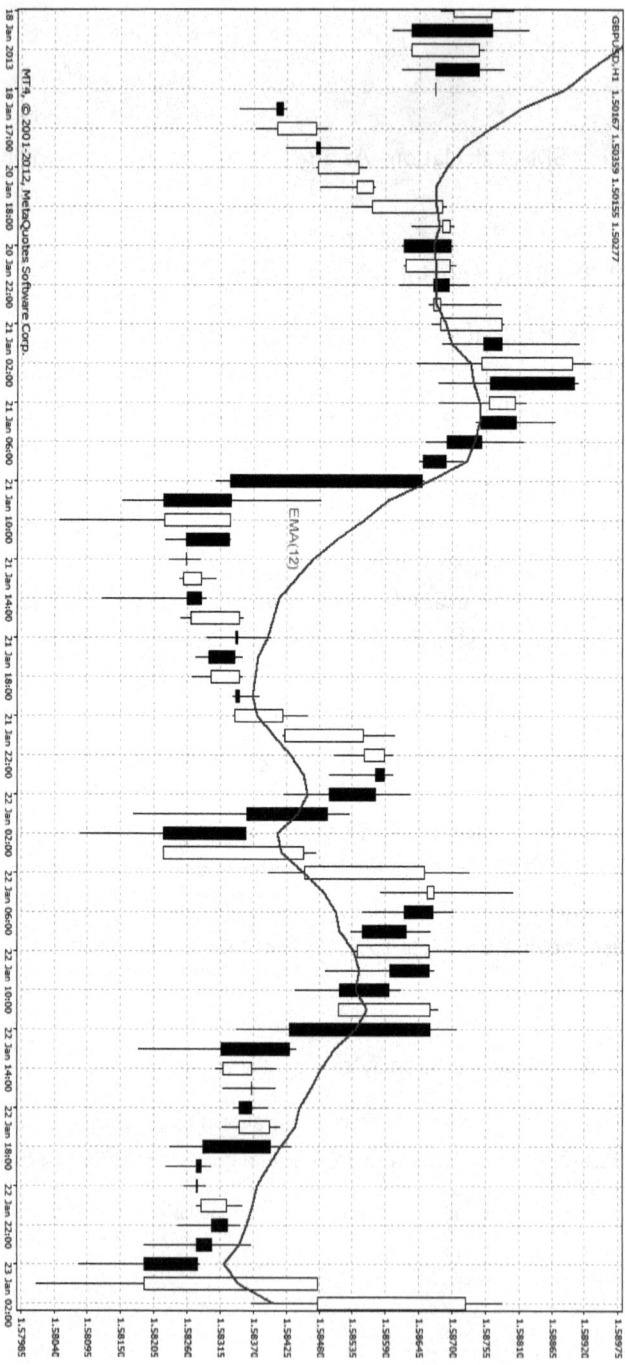

Figure 4.8: Example of an EMA(12) Indicator

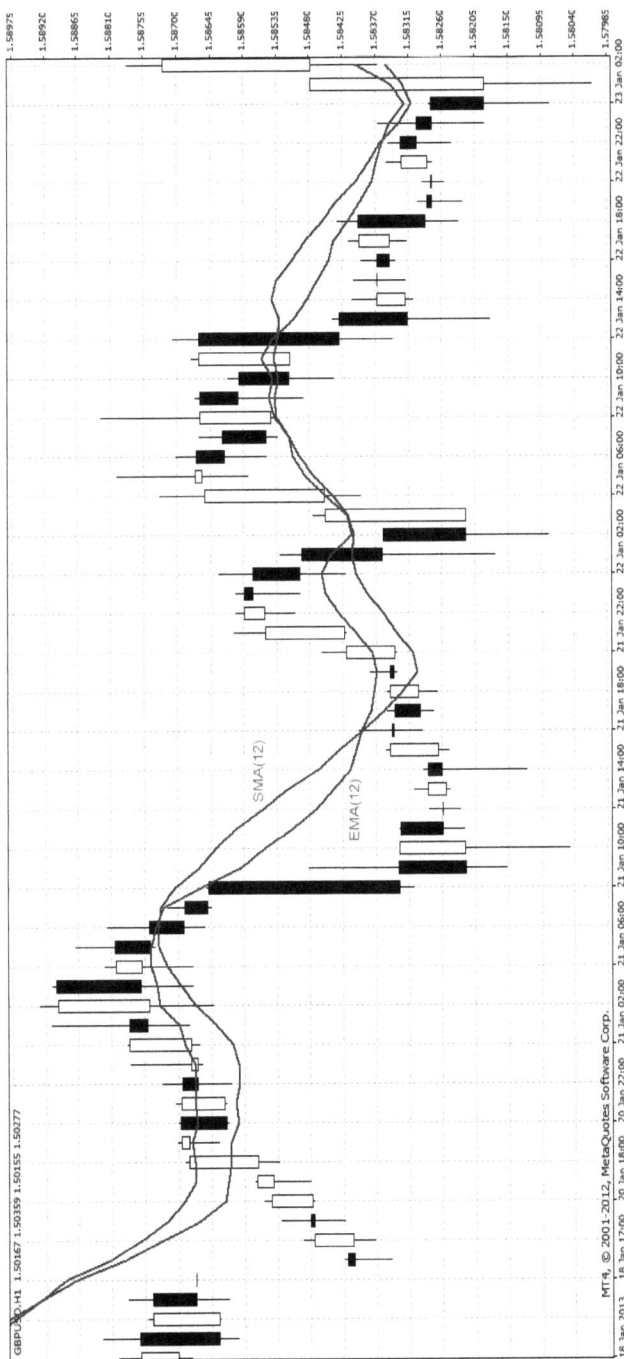

Figure 4.9: EMA(12) versus SMA(12)

you have one moving average crossing the other in order to be either above or below it. The advantage of using different periods for each moving average is that you can label them as either a *fast* or *slow* moving average:

- A *fast* moving average is the moving average with the smaller period size.

- A *slow* moving average is the moving average with the larger period size.

Fast moving averages follow closely to the actual close prices while slow moving averages take more time to change direction. For these reasons you normally see people use an SMA for the slow moving average and an EMA for the fast moving average. Popular choices for period sizes are 10 and 20, although this is definitely not set in stone. Figure 4.10 gives an example of what a moving average crossover looks like.

By using a fast and slow moving average, you can identify when a trend is changing direction by noticing when the two moving averages cross each other.

Moving Averages for Support/Resistance

Some people like to use the slow moving average as a line of support on an uptrend or a line of resistance on a downtrend. Personally I just like using them to measure crossover, but you should be aware of this alternate use.

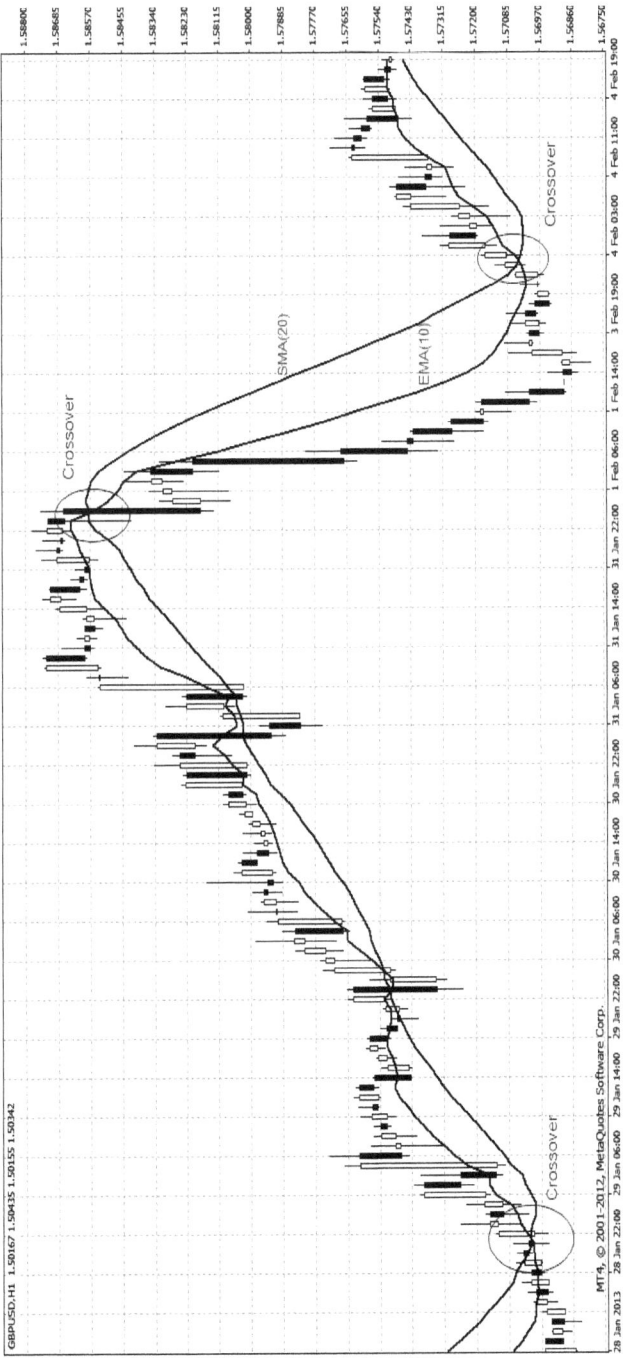

Figure 4.10: Example of an EMA(10)/SMA(20) Crossover

In Figure 4.10, there are a number of places where the two moving averages cross each other and each one is correlated with a change in the trend. Perfect! You now know how to make your millions! Well, almost. You are getting closer, but don't jump into the market just yet.

When do you actually buy or sell? Well, there are just a few rules you should follow to determine if you should buy or sell on a crossover:

1. If the fast moving average crosses above the slow moving average, the currency price is in an uptrend and this is considered to be a **Buy** signal.

2. If the fast moving average crosses below the slow moving average, the currency price is in a downtrend and this is considered to be a **Sell** signal.

3. If the difference between the fast and slow moving averages is small, i.e. less than 3 pips, wait for a few more candles to confirm the trend.

This last rule is one of my own, and it has saved me quite a few times over the years. Depending on the volatility of the currency you may be trading, these price fluctuations can easily drain your account if you traded every moving average cross. Let's take a quick look at a not-so-extreme example. Take a look at Figure 4.11. There are a few price fluctuations that trigger these "false" crossovers. If we had traded at each crossover, we would have lost quite a bit of money.

4.3 Summary

Using trend lines and moving averages you know how to spot a trend and see which direction it's headed in. Crossovers help identify when

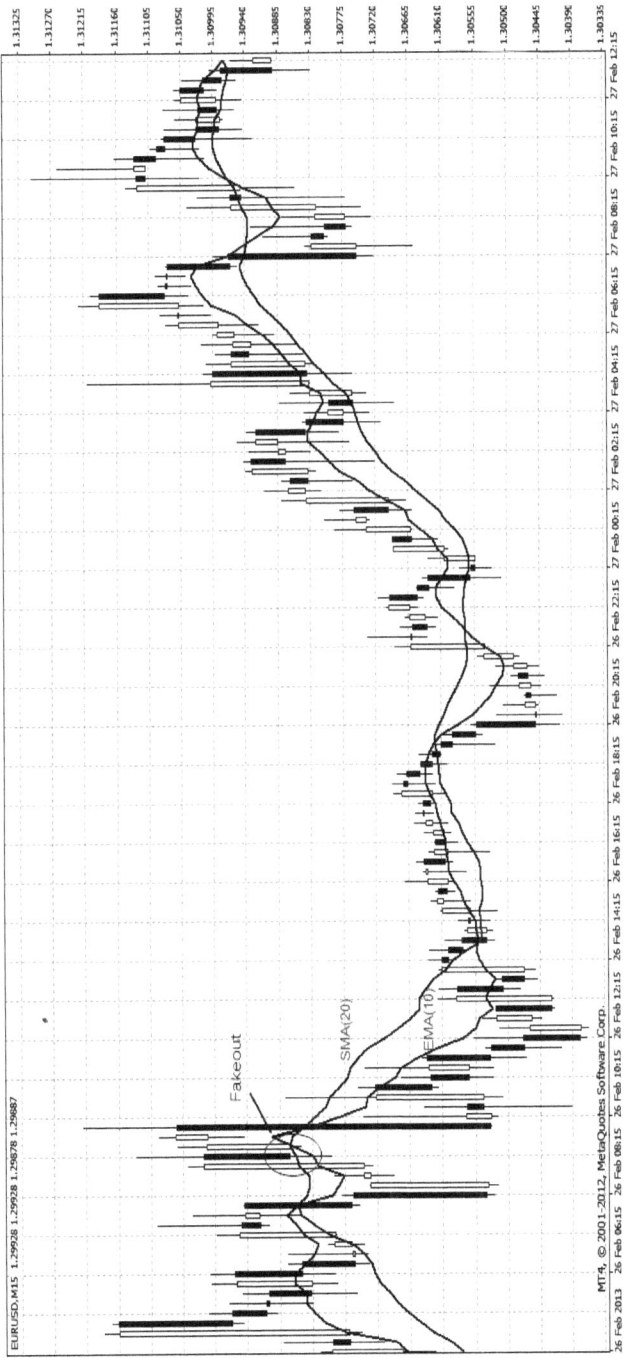

Figure 4.11: Volatile EMA(10)/SMA(20) Crossovers

a trend may be reversing, but don't be caught by the trend "faking" you out and going back in the original direction it was headed. These types of changes can grow to be costly, but there is a way to protect yourself from them. In the next chapter, we will look at some of the tools that can help identify true trend reversals from false ones.

CHAPTER 5

Moving With Momentum

As we saw in chapter 4 it is very easy to get caught off-guard with a trend as it reverses direction before you know what's happening. This can result in hitting your SL trigger rather quickly and also quickly empty your bank account. So what can we do? Turns out there are technical indicators to help with this too. They are not always foolproof (realistically nothing is or we would all be rich by now), but they do help to significantly reduce the risk of getting caught up in a false break-out.

We already know that the market has a natural up-and-down motion to the prices. This happens with all currencies traded on the Forex, with some being a little more wild than others. *Oscillators* can help identify this movement and help identify when the trend may be reversing. Oscillators also help to identify when a pair may be over-bought or oversold. Where moving averages and trend lines give us an indication of where the trend is now, oscillators can be used to help identify where the trend is going. Some people refer to oscillators as *leading* technical indicators, while moving averages are viewed as *lagging* indicators.

In this chapter we will be looking at a few different oscillators. They all serve the same purpose, but they go about doing it slightly differently. Remember that when you trade with technical indicators, you want to try to have about 3 - 4 indicators available that support one another. In Chapter 6 I will show you how to use most of the indicators introduced in this book to execute 20 days of trades.

So let's get started and dive into the first oscillator on our list - the *Relative Strength Index*.

5.1 Relative Strength Index (RSI)

The *Relative Strength Index (RSI)* is a simple momentum indicator that can be used to measure *over-bought* and *oversold* levels for a given pair. What are over-bought and oversold levels? We know that the price for a given pair will fluctuate, that is a given. If it wasn't, there would be no way for a Forex trader to make any money! What the RSI offers us is the ability to measure this price fluctuation and see when the price is too high (over-bought) or too low (oversold).

The RSI was created back in the late 1970s by J. Welles Wilder, and has been widely used ever since.

Who Is J. Welles Wilder?

J. Welles Wilder is an American mechanical engineer who is considered by most as one of the legendary technical indicator traders.

He invented a number of technical indicators including: *Relative Strength Index (RSI), Average True Range (ATR), Parabolic SAR* and more. The indicators he created back in the late 1970's are considered to be absolute staples in todays modern charting software packages. Without J. Welles Wilder, the Forex market would definitely be a harder market to understand and trade on. Thank you, Mr. Welles Wilder!

Let's take a look at how to use and interpret this indicator.

5.1.1   How To Use The RSI

Similar to moving averages, the RSI will measure prices over a given time period. Calculating the RSI returns a value between 0 and 100. Welles Wilder defined high and low "watermarks" for over-bought and oversold conditions at 70 and 30 respectively, and he recommended using a 14 period value for the calculation.

So what exactly does that mean? Well, if the RSI drops down below 30 then the currency pair is considered to be oversold and may be in a position to bounce back and have the price rise. Likewise if the RSI crosses above 70, then the currency pair is considered to be over-bought and a new sell-off may be coming.

As a stand-alone tool, the RSI is not very accurate. Combine it with a moving average and it can be used to help confirm or deny a trend reversal.

As we can see in Figure 5.1, this indicator can swing pretty rapidly! This is part of the reason why you should never rely on the RSI alone to interpret whether or not to buy or sell. One way in which I interpret

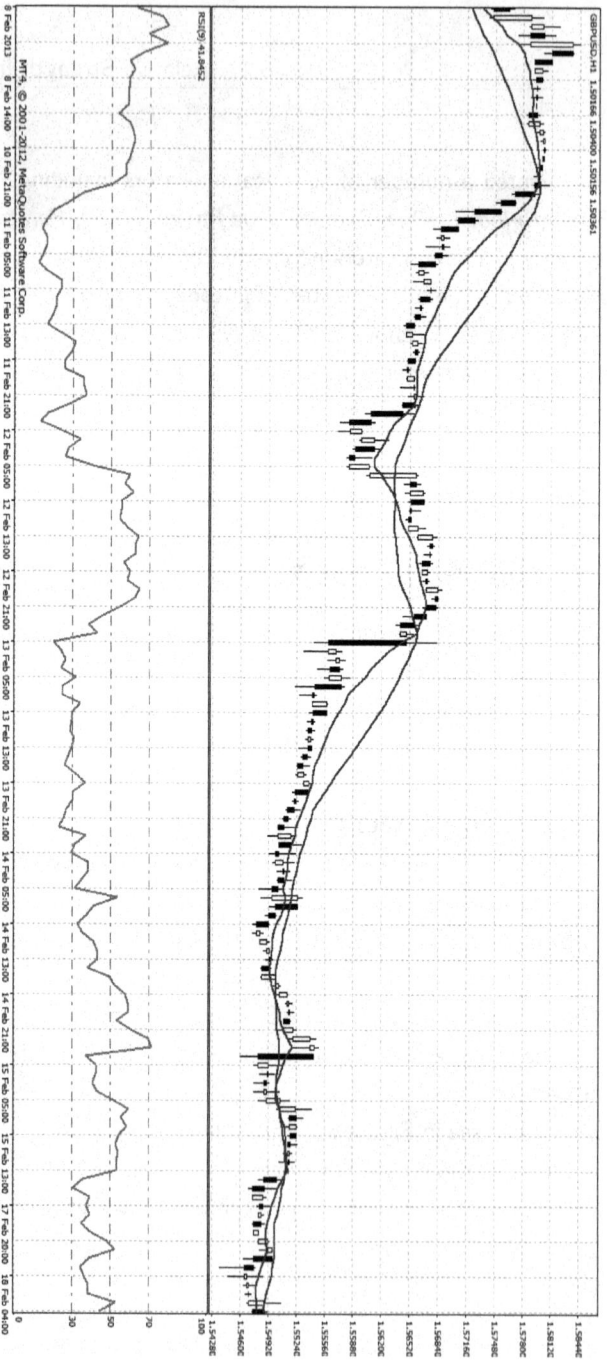

Figure 5.1: Relative Strength Index (RSI)

the RSI is to look for the RSI being between 50 and 70 when looking for a buy signal confirmation and between 30 and 50 when looking for a sell signal confirmation.

While the standard use of the RSI is to look for over-bought and oversold conditions, I personally have not had much success with this interpretation in the Forex market, so I would advise caution if that is the way that you want to interpret this indicator. Keep in mind that J. Welles Wilder created this indicator for trading stocks, not currencies.

5.1.2   Alternative Interpretations of the RSI

J. Welles Wilder originally suggested to use 14 periods when calculating the RSI with the over-bought and oversold levels at 70 and 30 respectively, some people have different views. Using a period size of 9 is fairly common in Forex[1], and some people set the over-bought/oversold levels at $80/20$ or even $90/10$.

As for myself, I find that RSI(9) with over-bought/oversold levels at $70/30$ work quite well, although that is always subject to change.

5.2   Stochastic Oscillator

Another popular momentum indicator is the *Stochastic Oscillator*. Similar to the RSI, this momentum indicator measures the closing price over a given time period. Compared to the RSI, the Stochastic Oscillator is definitely more involved. Take a look at Figure 5.2 to see the Stochastic Oscillator in action.

---

[1]Welles Wilder originally published his works for the stock market.

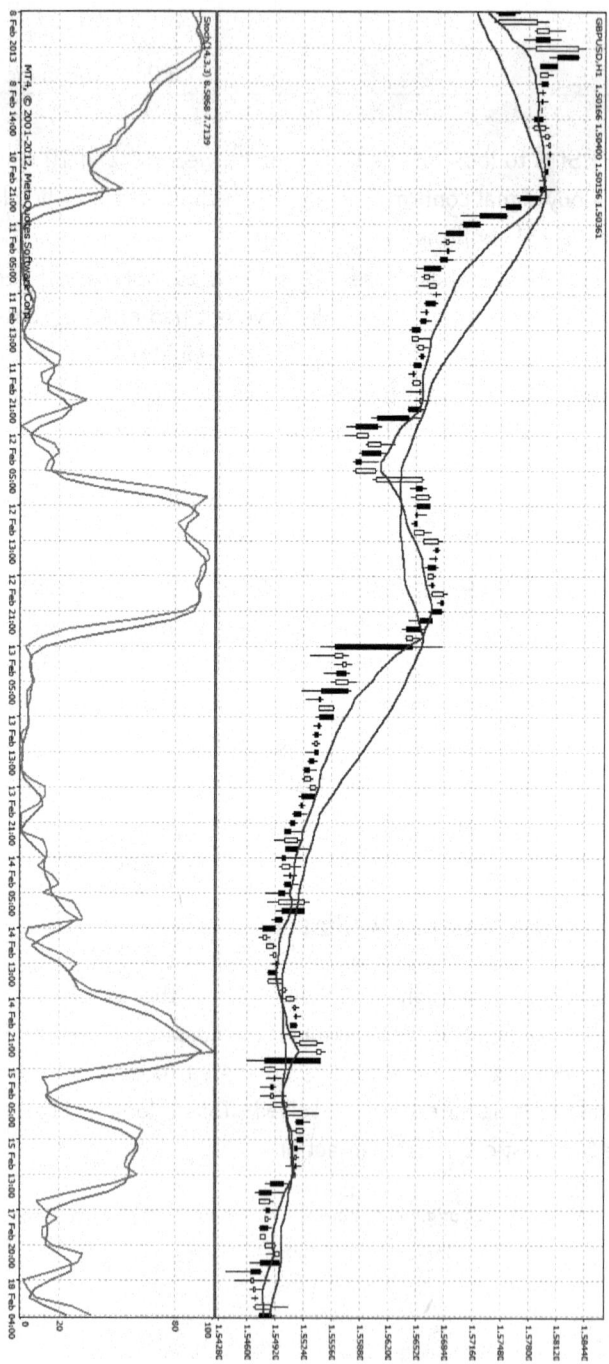

Figure 5.2: Stochastic Oscillator

The first thing you will notice is that there are two lines compared to the single line in the RSI. The two lines in the Stochastic are referred to as the *%K* and the *%D*. I'll be honest, it took me a while to get used to this one. The relationship between %K and %D is that %D is just a 3-period SMA of %K. It is just used to smooth out the %K line, which in and of itself is just a measure of the momentum for the price over the given number of periods.

5.2.1   How To Use The Stochastic Oscillator

Similar to the RSI, when you calculate the Stochastic both the %K and %D values will be between 0 and 100. Over-bought and oversold levels are set at 80 and 20 respectively, and the recommended period size is 14. You are usually able to specify the period size for the SMA used for determining %D, for which the default is 3.

There are essentially two ways to work with the Stochastic:

1. Use the same rules as the RSI, but use the %D line with the over-bought and oversold levels set to 80 and 20 respectively.

2. Use the crossover of the %K and %D the same way as a moving average crossover, where %K is the fast moving average and %D is the slow moving average.

A third option is to combine these two rules and require that the %K crosses the %D above or below the over-bought/oversold threshold to confirm another indicator's trend.

5.2.2   Variants of the Stochastic Oscillator

Some trading platforms offer multiple versions of the Stochastic Oscillator, namely the *Fast Stochastic*, *Slow Stochastic* or *Full Stochastic*.

The difference between the three is subtle, but important.

The *Fast Stochastic* is exactly as I have described previously.

The *Slow Stochastic* actually starts with the Fast Stochastic, but then uses the %D value of the Fast Stochastic and uses it as the Slow Stochastic's %K. The Slow Stochastic will use SMA(3) to calculate the %K value, and then use the specified period size for the SMA to calculate the Slow Stochastic's %D. Confused yet? Don't worry, it all boils down to both the %K and %D lines being smoother than the equivalent Fast Stochastic.

The *Full Stochastic* works exactly the same as the Slow Stochastic, except you can specify all three parameters:

- The period size for the oscillator
- The period size for the SMA used for calculating %K
- The period size for the SMA used for calculating %D

The default values are normally 14, 3 and 3 for each of these properties respectively.

So which one should you use? It's actually a personal preference, and it may be limited by your trading software. If you have an option, I would use the Full Stochastic. The extra smoothing helps to weed out some choppiness and potential false signals. The default values of 14, 3, 3 are sufficient, but you may want to try changing these values to see how the system behaves and to fit your own needs.

5.3   Moving Average Convergence Divergence (MACD)

The final momentum technical indicator that I will cover is the *Moving Average Convergence Divergence*, or *MACD* for short. It is another momentum indicator that tracks the relationship between two moving averages.   In essence it is similar to the moving average crossover strategy I discussed earlier, but rather than plotting a moving average of the price, it is actually plotting the moving average of the *difference* of the moving average of the price. What that boils down to is that the MACD reacts fairly slowly compared to using moving averages on their own.

Investopedia[2] defines the MACD as:

> A trend-following momentum indicator that shows the re-
> lationship between two moving averages of prices. The
> MACD is calculated by subtracting the 26-day exponential
> moving average (EMA) from the 12-day EMA. A nine-day
> EMA of the MACD, called the "signal line", is then plot-
> ted on top of the MACD, functioning as a trigger for buy
> and sell signals.

Figure 5.3 gives an example of the MACD.

The bars in the MACD graph are just a representation of the dif-ference between the two graphs, and can provide a simple way to know when the MACD is higher than the 9-period EMA (the bars are above zero) or lower than the 9-period EMA (the bars are below zero). The MACD does not have any upper or lower limits like the RSI and Stochastic Oscillator do. The *MACD* line plots the difference between *EMA(26)* and *EMA(12)*. The *signal line* is simply the plot of EMA(9) of the MACD line. Finally the *trigger line* is the zero line of the chart, i.e. where the value for any chart value is zero.

---

[2]Read more: http://www.investopedia.com/terms/m/macd.asp#ixzz2MO07Zxha

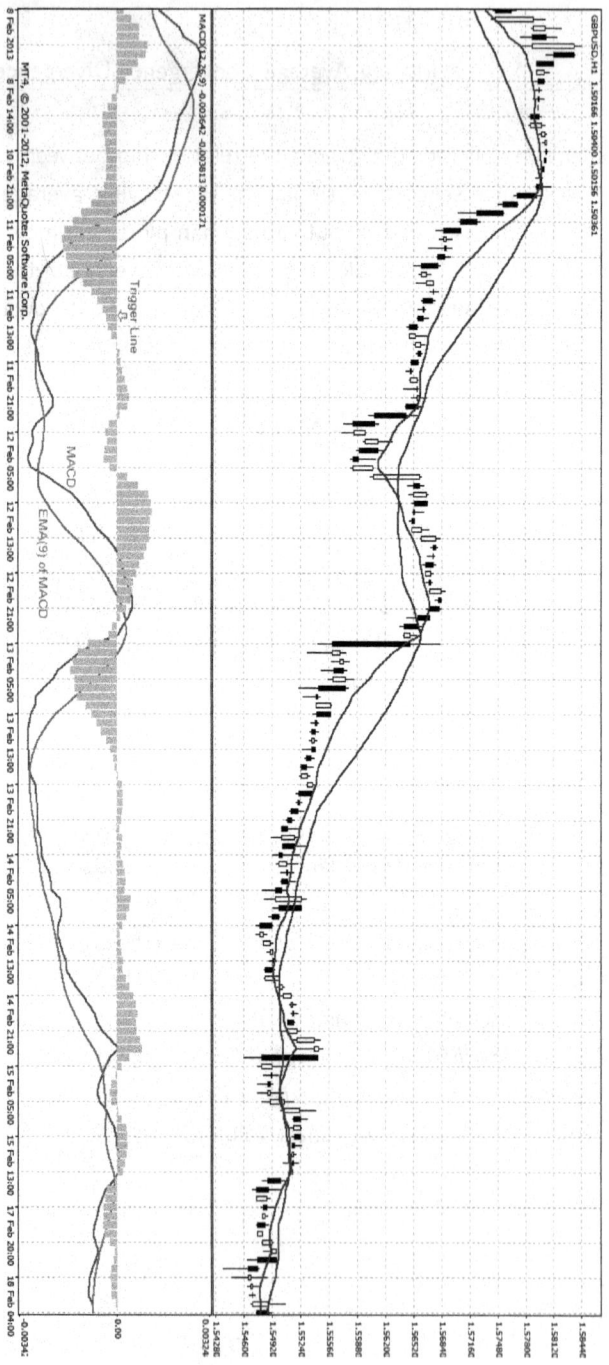

Figure 5.3: Moving Average Convergence Divergence (MACD)

5.3.1 How To Use The MACD

There are three ways to interpret the MACD:

- When the trigger line is crossed.

- When the moving averages cross.

- When the MACD line goes in the opposite direction of the market trend.

The first two methods are similar; when the MACD line crosses the trigger line or the 9-period EMA, then depending on how it crosses that would indicate a *Buy* or *Sell* signal. For the trigger line, the MACD crosses above the trigger line then that would be regarded as a *Buy* signal. If it crosses below the trigger line then that is considered a *Sell* signal.

The interpretation for the moving averages crossing is a little more involved. If the MACD line crosses above the 9-period EMA **and** both lines are **below** the trigger line, then that can be interpreted as a *Buy* signal. If the MACD line crosses below the 9-period EMA **and** both lines are **above** the trigger line, then that can be interpreted as a *Sell* signal.

The last interpretation can be viewed as an "early warning system" for a trend reversal, but I would personally recommend against using this interpretation until you get a lot of practice with the MACD. The reason being is that it relies on you knowing what the trend currently is, and then notice that the MACD is going in the opposite direction. However there is no guarantee that the trend will actually reverse, so it can put you in a bad spot. My suggestion for this last type of interpretation is to follow its advice *if and only if* you want to close out a trade earlier than you normally would and closing out the trade will result in a profit for you.

5.4 Summary

Momentum indicators are a must-have tool in your trading toolbox. Without them, it is very easy to get caught on the wrong side of a trend. Using them on their own will leave you depressed, angry and poor. However when you combine them with something like a pair of moving averages, you can greatly increase your chances of making some good profits!

In the next chapter I will show you how all these concepts and indicators can work together allowing you to make some successful trades.

CHAPTER 6

20 Days of Trading

One of my biggest issues with most Forex books is that they throw a lot of concepts and indicators at you, show you some charts that show how those indicators and concepts fit perfectly and then expect you to know enough to go out and do it all on your own. I am not a fan of this approach for two reasons. First, in the real world it is almost never that easy. Second, often times the indicators that they show are using multiple time periods (some are one hour, others are 15 minutes, etc) so they are not consistent, leaving no explanation to the reader on how to get these indicators working for the pair that they would like to trade.

Thankfully this is not one of those books. In this chapter we will be trading the NZD/USD pair for the month of December, 2012 on a 1 hour (H1) chart. Why this pair? I personally find it rather stable and easy to find trends on, both of which are key for a first-time trader. This pair has a PIP spread of 2 PIPs, so we will account for that in our trades when executing and closing orders. Let us take a look at the financial details for this exercise - what we are going to start with and how we are going to manage our risk.

6.1 Financial Information

I will be working with an account that has $5,000 USD in it, trading with a 30:1 leverage. This gives me a working balance of $150,000 USD, or approximately 15 mini lots. While micro lots are an option as well, I like to trade mini lots since it makes the math a bit easier when determining your profit. Since we are trading the NZD/USD with mini lots, 1 PIP is equivalent to $1 USD.

6.2 Risk Management

As far as money management is concerned, I will try to use the 2% rule. The 2% rule basically means that for any single trade, you should not risk more than 2% of your available capital. This means that even if you have a few bad trades, you are not going to lose all your money. So what does it mean for me? Given the current leverage and the fact that I am using mini lots, a single lot would put me closer to 6.67% of my initial capital. I am willing to take that risk, so we will be trading with one mini lot for each order. This could increase over time as my account balance grows, but to keep things simple I will be sticking to a single mini lot for all the trades done in this chapter.

6.3   Tools of The Trade

There are a lot of different tools available to a technical Forex trader. Chapters 4 and 5 covered only a small number of these that I have found useful over the years. Often times when a new trader opens up their trading software, they see dozens of different tools available at their disposal, and are either incredibly excited or incredibly scared because of the sheer number of these tools. The term "analysis paralysis" is often used when describing someone who is completely overwhelmed with technical indicator tools by either not knowing which ones to use or by trying to use all of them. I find that $2 - 4$ of these tools work best. Finding which ones to use is often a personal choice.

I will keep things simple and use two moving averages; an exponential moving average over 11 periods and a simple moving average over 19 periods. I will refer to these as EMA(11) and SMA(19) for the remainder of this chapter. I will also be using a Relative Strength Indicator (RSI) over 9 periods, also referred to as RSI(9) for the remainder of this chapter. The goal will be to look for trend changes when the moving averages cross over, but we will be looking at the RSI(9) to indicate support for the trend.

The first question you should be asking is why did I pick EMA(11), SMA(19) and RSI(9)? Some seasoned traders will use EMA(10) and SMA(20), but I like prime numbers more. RSI(14) is the "standard" setup, but RSI(9) is another popular choice. Personally I like RSI(9) more than RSI(14) based on past results, so that is why I chose it. There are no hard-and-fast numbers that will work all the time for every pair. These indicators are what I chose, but it does not mean that they are the "correct" ones, if there are any at all. Remember to keep a trade log and try to find indicators that work best for you. Experiment with a practice account and try to keep track of what works for you on whatever pair you choose to trade.

6.3.1 Indicator Rules

We have our tools chosen for us, but we should still have a set of rules in place so that we know what action to take when something happens with our indicators. Here is the list of rules that I will be following:

- If EMA(11) > SMA(19), this is a Buy signal
- If EMA(11) < SMA(19), this is a Sell signal
- The delta (or absolute difference) between the values of EMA(11) and SMA(19) must be >= 3.5 pips in order to further evaluate the signal
- If the moving averages cross and indicate a buy signal, then RSI(9) must also be between 50 and 70
- If the moving averages cross and indicate a sell signal, then RSI(9) must also be between 30 and 50
- A Stop Loss trigger will be set 50 pips from the opening (or strike) price of the order
- A Take Profit trigger will be set 250 pips above the strike price[1]

These are the main rules that we will follow. Since the pair can change at any moment, we will exercise some discretion as we execute our trades to make sure these rules line up properly for us.

Remember that emotion is a huge part of trading and the biggest hurdle to overcome for a new trader, especially with live accounts.

---

[1] This gives a risk-reward ratio of 1 : 5

Having rules in place can help quite a bit since they give you something to follow. Using a longer time period for trading also makes it easier to focus on the trends and not get caught up in small movements where you start to second-guess yourself. We will see an example of this below.

6.4 Bob's Trading Adventure

Without further delay, let us begin our trading of the NZD/USD[2]!

I will be presenting the following 20 days in the role of Bob, who has read the previous chapters but is still a novice trader with a day job. Bob will not be able to watch the pair price all day. Bob has traded on a practice accounts for six months, so he knows how the Forex market works but he has only traded with real money for the last three months. A lot of the comments Bob will make are similar to how I felt when I first started trading, but I am not necessarily basing Bob on myself. The goal here is to show *how* to trade using the tools provided, rather than a mini-autobiography.

The trading day will start at 07:00 each morning, Monday through Friday. Bob will stop monitoring at 23:00 each night, except for Fridays when he stops at 17:00. That is when the last market, New York, closes for the weekend.

While the Forex does technically open on Sunday, Bob wants to keep his weekend free. Also it helps to let the market decide what it wants to do in the first few hours when it opens on Sunday, which is

---

[2]All the dates and times given are in Eastern Standard Time (EST), just so we are on the same page.

a safer approach for Bob rather than jumping in right away when it first opens.

Since Bob cannot afford to watch the currency price all day long, he will be using a 1 hour (H1) chart when determining what action to take. As he finds time throughout the day, he will look and see how things are progressing. Charts will be provided for each day and should be referenced as you read about Bob's journey.

Now that we have all of this prep work out of the way, let's get started.

6.4.1   Day 1 - December 3, 2012

> "Day 1. I just woke up I'm ready to start trading! Let me take a quick look to see how NZD/USD is doing."

Bob takes a look at the H1 chart for NZD/USD, as can be seen in Figure 6.1.

> "Interesting, there seems to be a trend underway! Let me check the technical indicators to see how they line up against my trading rules."

This is pretty exciting since it's not always the case that you find a trend when you first start trading[3]. Bob continues to evaluate the technical indicators he has plotted with the rules from Section 6.3.1:

- "EMA(11) is 0.82021, and SMA(19) is 0.81983, giving a delta of 3.8 pips[4]. That meets the minimum required delta value of 3.5 pips."

---

[3] I am a big fan of holding back and waiting for a new trend to start rather than trying to catch one that has already started.

[4] $(0.82021 - 0.81983) * 10000 = 3.8$

88

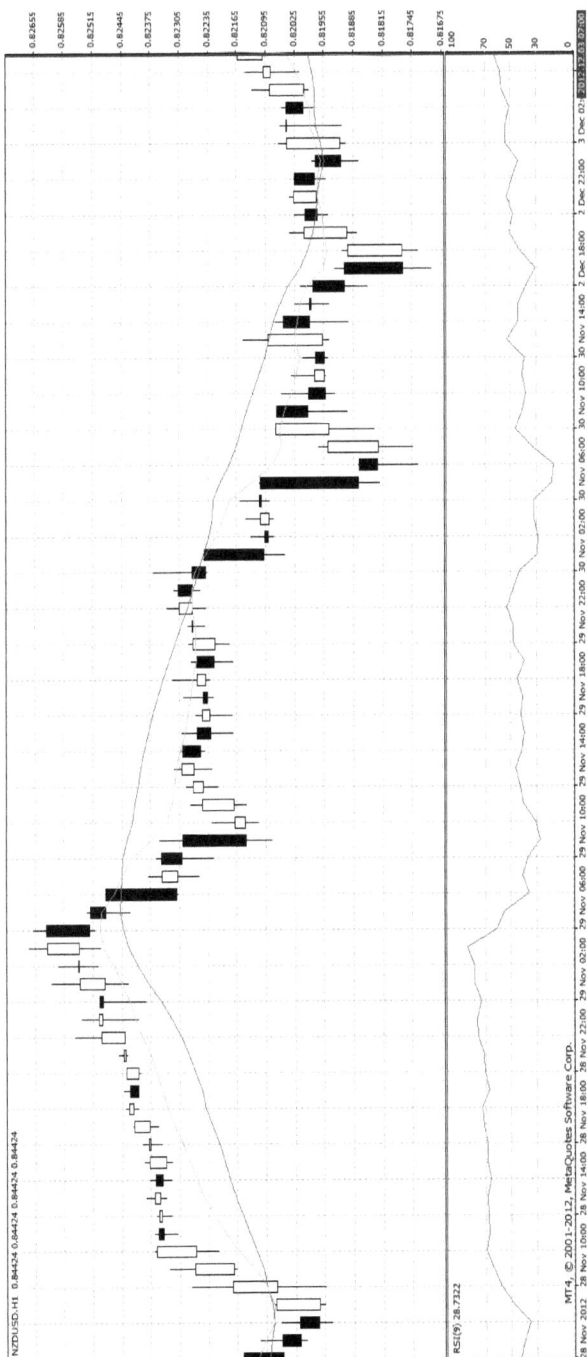

Figure 6.1: December 3, 2012 at 07:00

- "EMA(11) is higher than SMA(19), indicating a buy signal."

- "RSI(9) is 58.496, which is between 50 and 70, so the RSI(9) confirms the buy signal."

"The rules say that I should open a Buy order, so that's exactly what I'm going to do."

Bob places a *Buy* order for 1 mini-lot and opens the order with a price of 0.82112. He sets a stop-loss (SL) trigger at 0.81612 and a take-profit (TP) trigger at 0.84612. Bob checks the chart at 12:00 to see if anything has changed, but the trend direction remains the same. When Bob gets home at 18:00, he checks the chart again to see if there is any change.

"It looks like the moving averages are starting to converge. I'll keep an eye on these for the next few hours to see if I should switch positions."

Bob continues to monitor the charts for the next few hours.

"It looks like there was some activity that was causing the moving averages to cross over quite a bit but not enough to meet the minimum delta rule. RSI(9) was also hovering around 50, so that tells me that these crossovers may just be false signals."

By the time 23:00 hits, the original buy trend is still holding so he decides to call it a day and heads off to bed. Figure 6.2 shows the activity for the day.

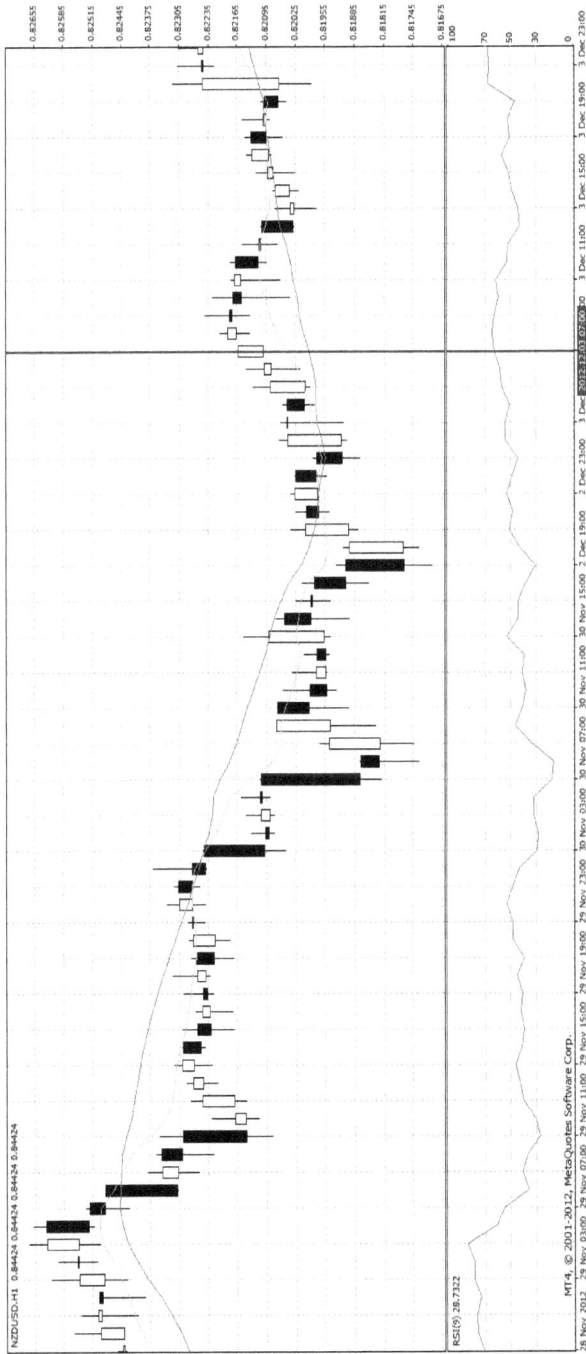

Figure 6.2: December 3, 2012 at 23:00

6.4.2 Day 2 - December 4, 2012

At 07:00, Bob gets up and takes a look at the H1 chart to see how his trade is performing. Figure 6.3 is the chart Bob looks at.

> "Looks good! The trend is still strong and it looks like I'm starting to make a profit. I am tempted to cash out now and just take what I can get, but I have a good feeling about this one."

This is a common trap that most new traders fall into, namely the desire for quick profits. While there is nothing wrong with that, I still consider it a trap since you will not make as much money compared to if you hold on to your trade - provided that the indicators support it. Taking a profit early and then re-entering the trade means that you will be hit with the pip spread again. Depending on when you time your exits and entries, it may start to cost you more than you expected. This is especially true if you exit and re-enter just before a reversal. Keep an eye on the indicators and act accordingly. Unless you have a hard target you want to hit, then I would encourage you to hold on to the trend as much as possible. If your TP trigger is hit, then take it and be thankful. If it hasn't hit and the indicators do not show a reversal, then I would not quit early. Of course this is not fool-proof since something like bad GDP earnings, high jobless rate or something similar may cause a sudden reversal in the trend.

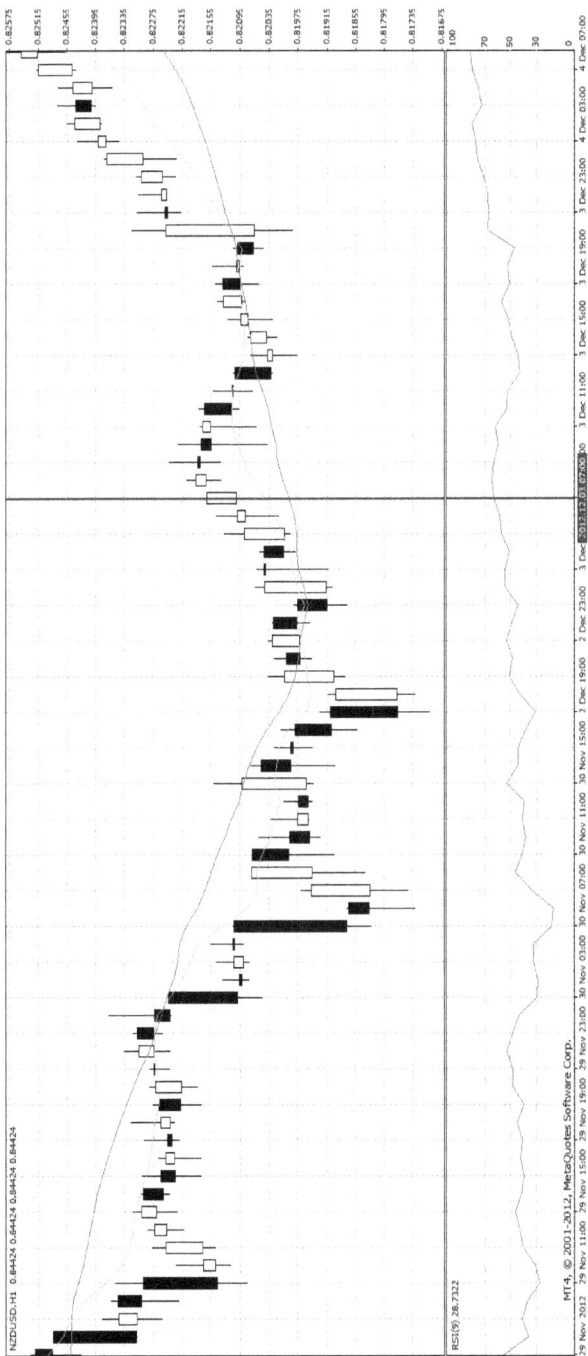

Figure 6.3: December 4, 2012 at 07:00

"The trend is still strong and RSI(9) hasn't reached an
overbought[5] level yet, so I'll leave things well enough alone
for now. I'll check things again when I'm at the office."

Bob checks the chart again at 13:00, but the trend continues as do
his profits so Bob waits until 18:00 to check the chart again.

"Interesting, there seems to have been a small crossover
in the moving averages!"

Bob continues to monitor until 23:00, but the moving averages crossover
again and resume the original trend. The delta was never close to the
minimum of 3.5 pips, so there was never a need to switch his position
from Buy to Sell. Figure 6.4 shows what the pair price looked like for
the rest of the day.

6.4.3   Day 3 - December 5, 2012

Bob wakes up at 07:00 on day 3 of his 20 day trading adventure and
quickly looks at the H1 chart as shown in Figure 6.5.

"The markets were pretty quiet overnight, it seems. I see
no reason to change anything. I'm definitely past the *day
trader* moniker now, since I'm on day 3 of having an open
order."

Bob checks the chart again at 14:00 and notices that the trend seems
to be slowing down as the moving averages are running parallel to
each other. At 18:00, Bob checks the chart again.

"Wow! At 15:00 there was some serious upwards pressure
on the pair, strengthening my position! This is great news,
since I've earned quite a few more pips!"

---

[5]Normally a value above 80 can be considered over bought and a value below
20 is considered oversold.

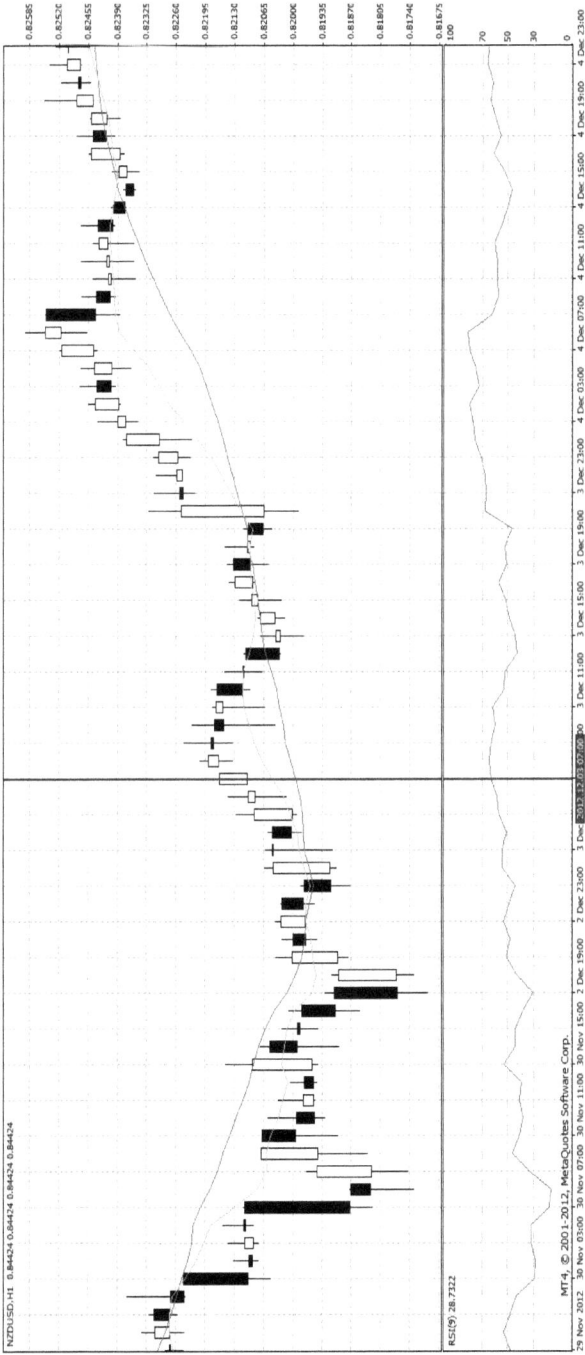

Figure 6.4: December 4, 2012 at 23:00

Figure 6.5: December 5, 2012 at 07:00

The trend continues upwards for Bob and at 23:00, he takes one last look at the chart as seen in Figure 6.6, sees that the trend is continuing in his favor, and heads to bed.

6.4.4 Day 4 - December 6, 2012

Bob wakes up at 07:00, anxious to look at the NZD/USD H1 chart. Figure 6.7 illustrates what he sees.

> "Things are still on the up-and-up as far as the trend is concerned. Great news for me!"

Bob continues to watch the H1 chart during the day. When he arrives home at 18:00, he notices that there was a big drop at 15:00. Bob is concerned, since it looks like this drop has erased the gains from the previous 2 hours. However the moving averages have not crossed over yet. Bob continues to monitor the price until 01:00, at which point he decides to trust his SL and TP triggers and heads off to bed. Figure 6.8 gives a depiction of what he saw during this time.

> "Well, there was definitely a big drop that happened at 17:00. It seemed to have erased the gains from the previous two hours, so I decided to watch it for a while to see if the trend was headed for a reverse. After watching the trend for a few more hours I decide to call it a night at around 01:00. There was a small crossover around 22:00, but the delta wasn't large enough to close my order. The fact that RSI(9) was very close to 50 since 17:00 helped, as it served as another confirmation that this might be a false breakout. I decide to go to bed, but I do anxiously await the morning."

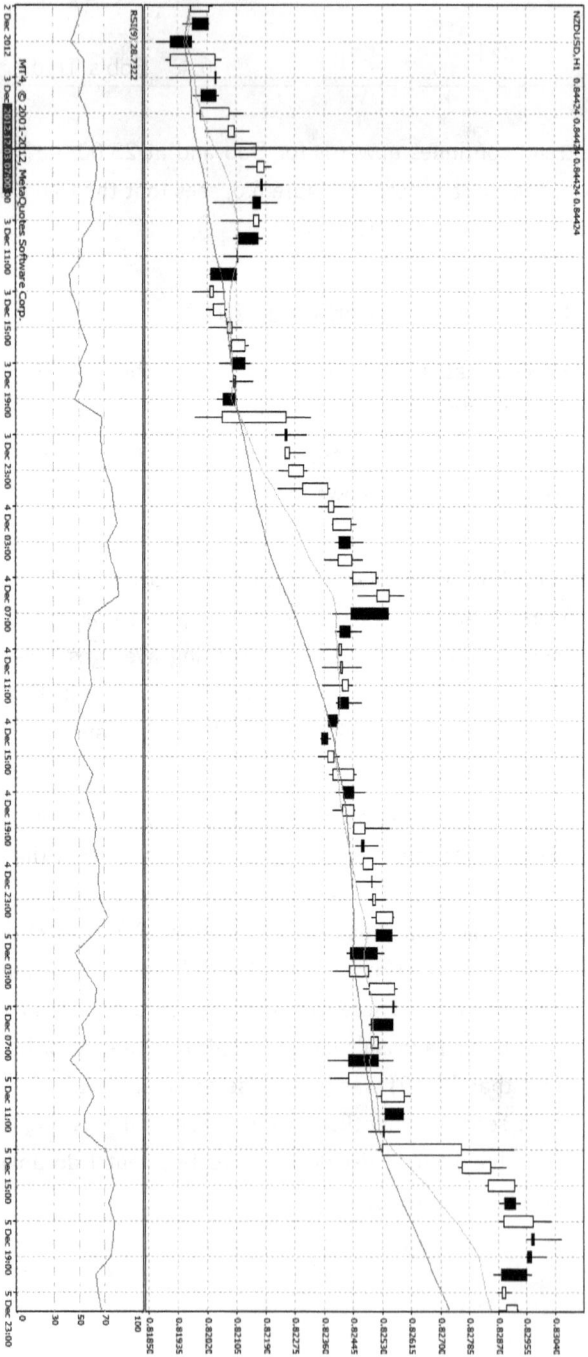

Figure 6.6: December 5, 2012 at 23:00

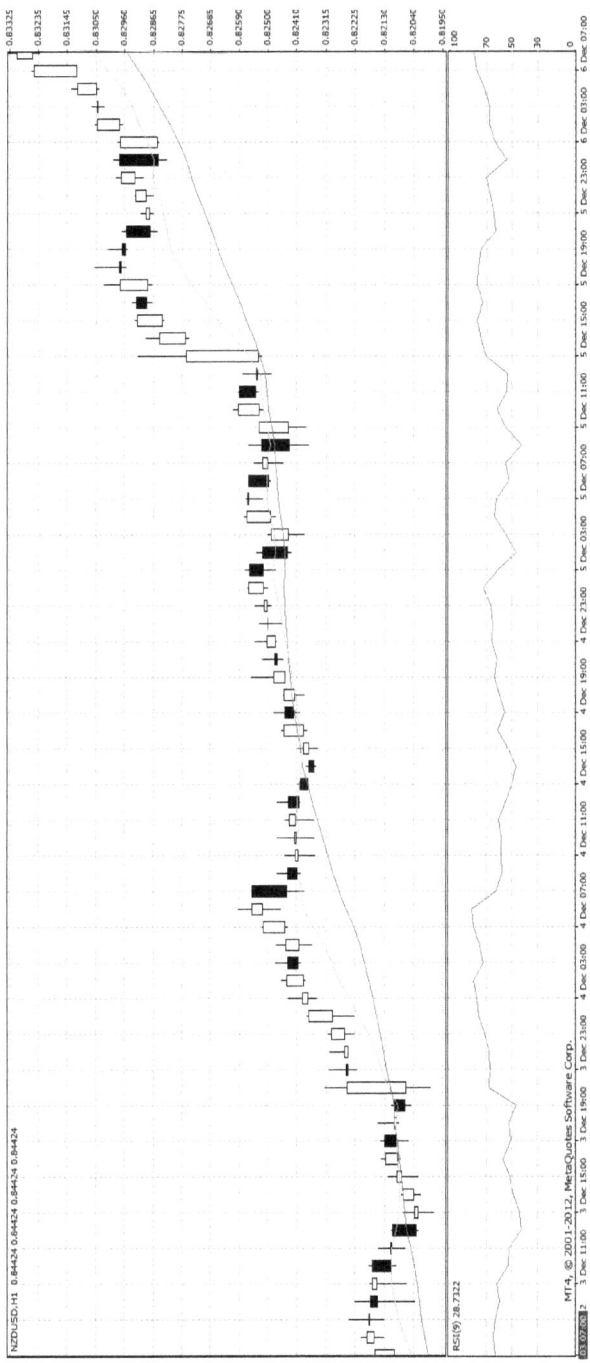

Figure 6.7: December 6, 2012 at 07:00

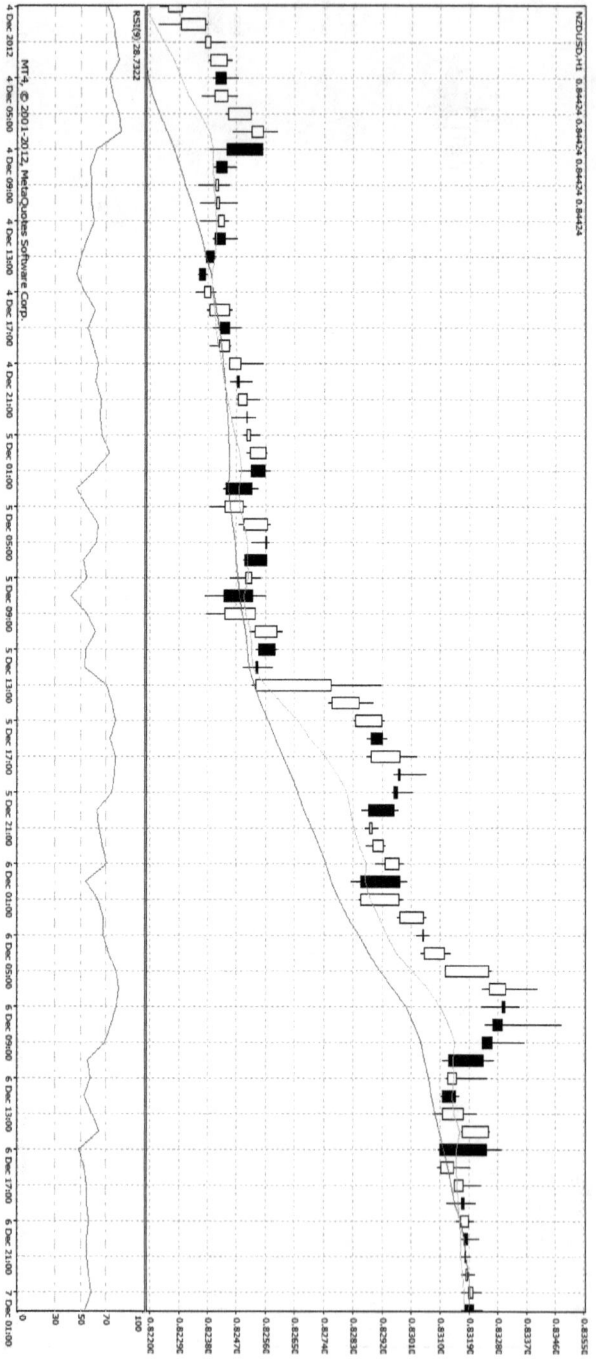

Figure 6.8: December 7, 2012 at 01:00

6.4.5 Day 5 - December 7, 2012

Friday comes and Bob prepares for a shorter trading day. At 07:00, he checks the H1 chart to see what the overnight price movement was like.

> "I know from reading Forex books and websites that Friday's are generally when big players cash out of their positions to take whatever profits they can for the week. I'm expecting that the trend has reversed."

Figure 6.9 is what Bob sees at 07:00.

> "Well, the market certainly is struggling to make up its mind! The moving averages have crossed over, but once again the delta is not nearly large enough to do anything about it. I'll definitely be keeping an eye on this at work."

Bob continues to monitor the H1 chart at the office. By the time 17:00 rolls around, Bob sees no reason to close his order before the weekend. Figure 6.10 shows the day 5 chart as of 17:00.

> "Watching the chart a few times during the day gave me no insight. I look at the chart at 16:00, giving me an hour to decide before the market closes for the weekend. The trend seems to be continuing, so I decide to leave my order alone. One last check at 17:00 shows that RSI(9) is sitting near 50, so I feel comfortable leaving my order open over the weekend."

6.4.6 Day 6 - December 10, 2012

Bob kept to his word and didn't look at the NZD/USD chart at all on Sunday. At 07:00, he woke up and saw the same chart as Figure 6.11.

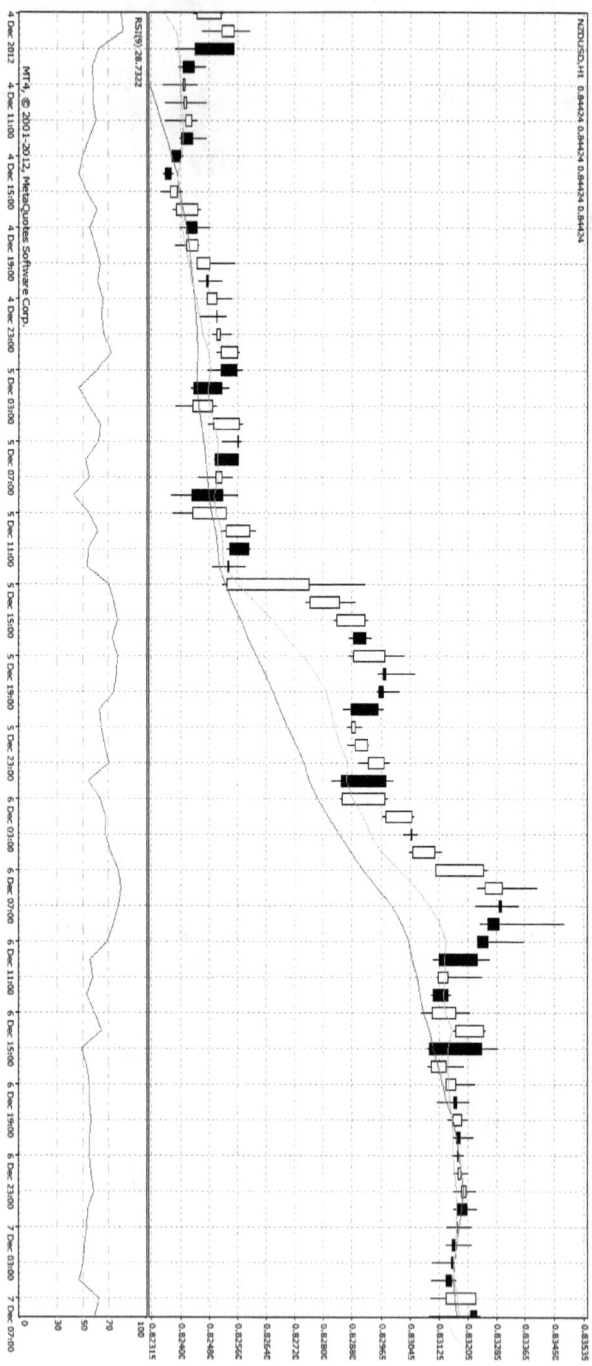

Figure 6.9: December 7, 2012 at 07:00

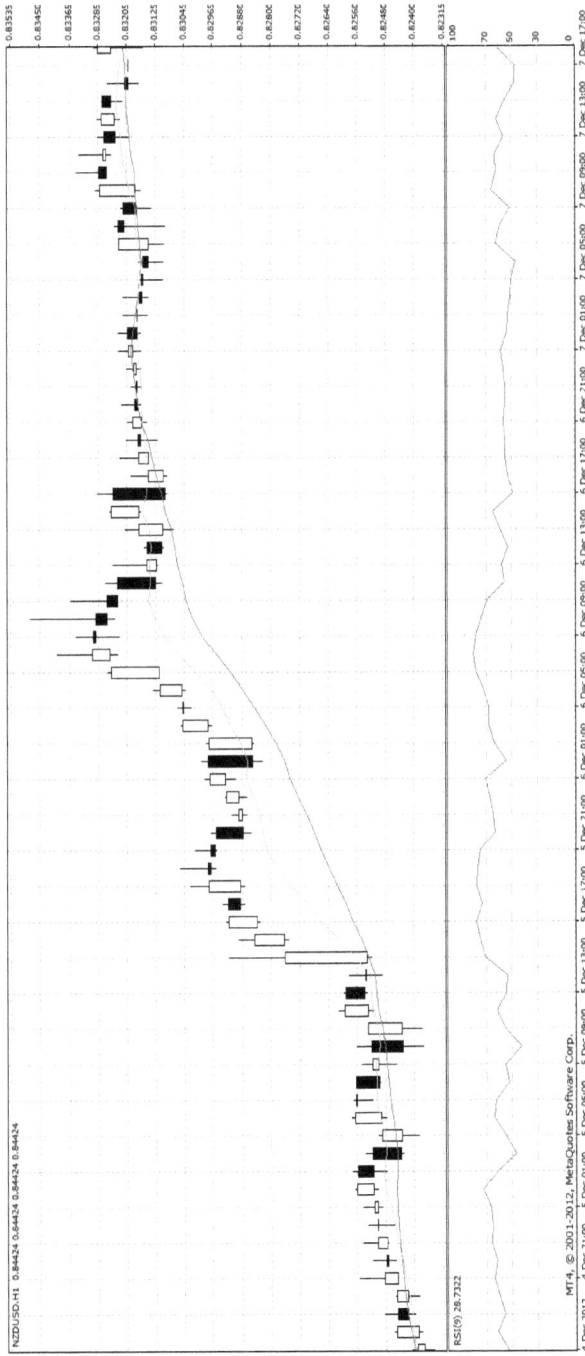

Figure 6.10: December 7, 2012 at 17:00

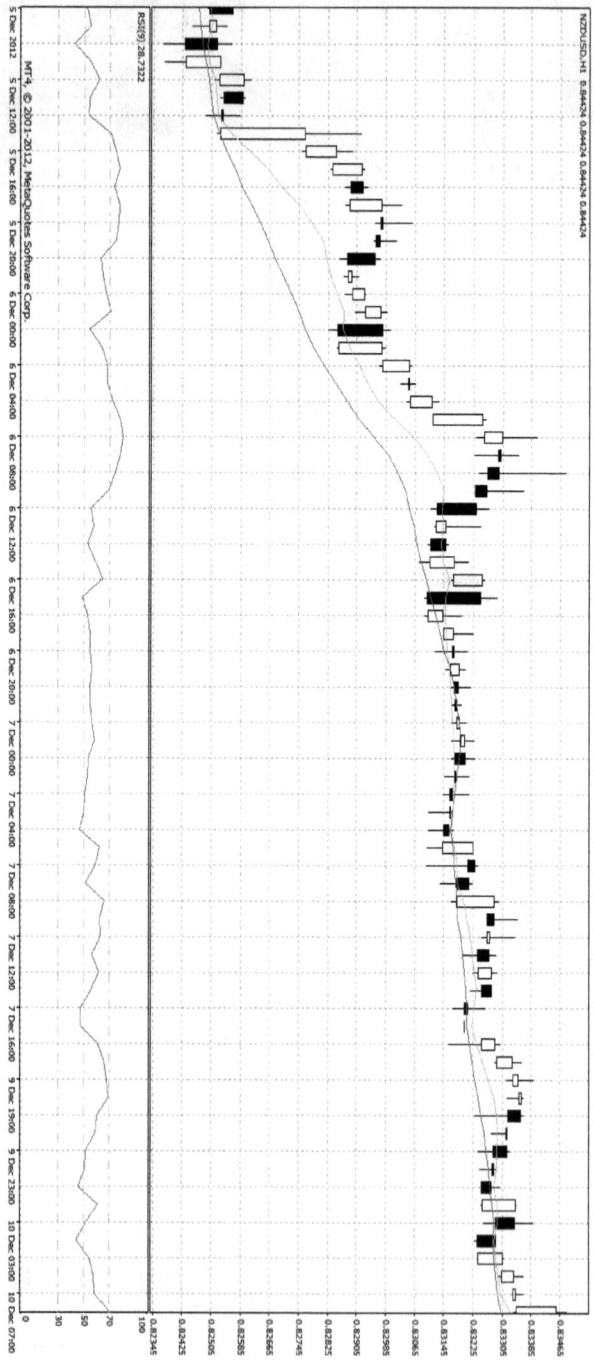

Figure 6.11: December 10, 2012 at 07:00

"No change. There was some minor squeezing of the moving averages around 04:00, but that has since expanded. Nice to see this trend continuing!"

Bob heads in for work and checks on the chart throughout the day. Figure 6.12 is what he sees at 23:00 before heading off to bed.

6.4.7 Day 7 - December 11, 2012

Another day and Bob looks over his order. Figure 6.13 shows the day 7 chart at 07:00.

"Looks like there is good continued upward movement. I haven't seen the pinching of the moving averages for a while, so I'm wondering if the bears[6] in the market are hibernating. For now the trade looks strong, so I'm going to let it ride for a while."

The trend continues strongly for Bob right up to 23:00. Figure 6.14 shows the 23:00 chart and he sees the trend continuing.

6.4.8 Day 8 - December 12, 2012

Day 8, and Figure 6.15 shows what Bob sees at 07:00. The trend continued overnight, making Bob pretty excited. At 07:00 the price is hovering around 0.84087, meaning Bob is up $(0.84087 - 0.82112) \times 10000 = 197.5$ pips! Very exciting!

As Bob checks through the day, the trend continues to hold steady right up to 23:00, as can be see by Figure 6.16.

---

[6]Remember that a *bear* market is downward trending market.

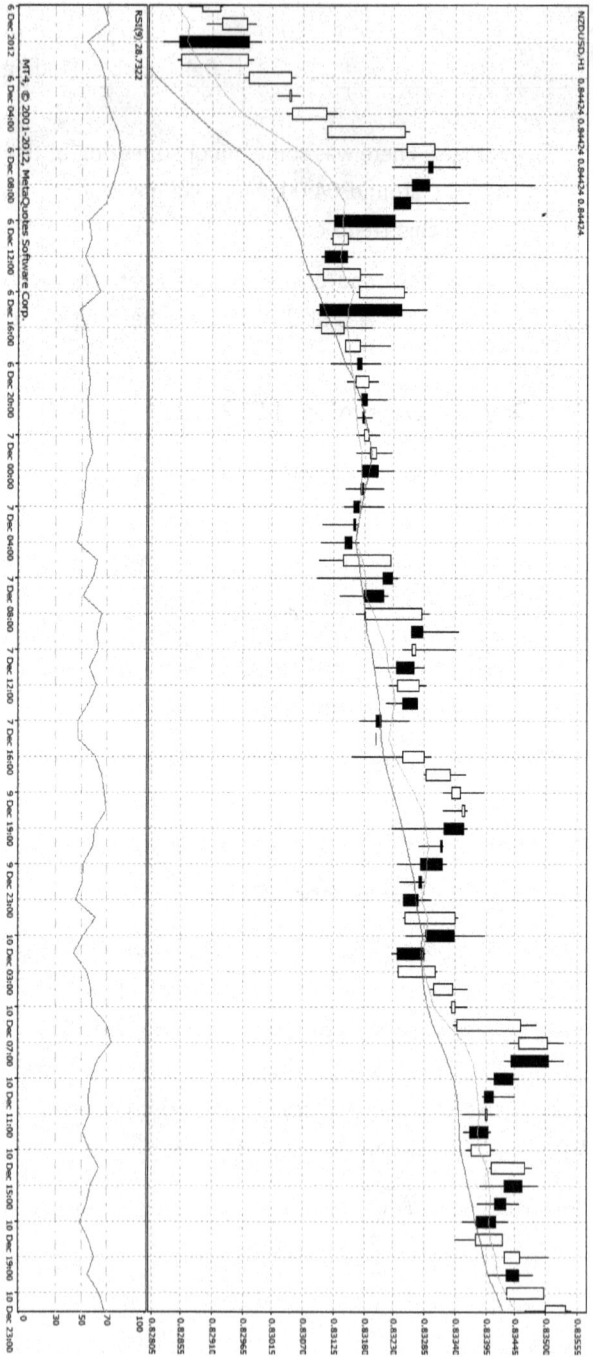

Figure 6.12: December 10, 2012 at 23:00

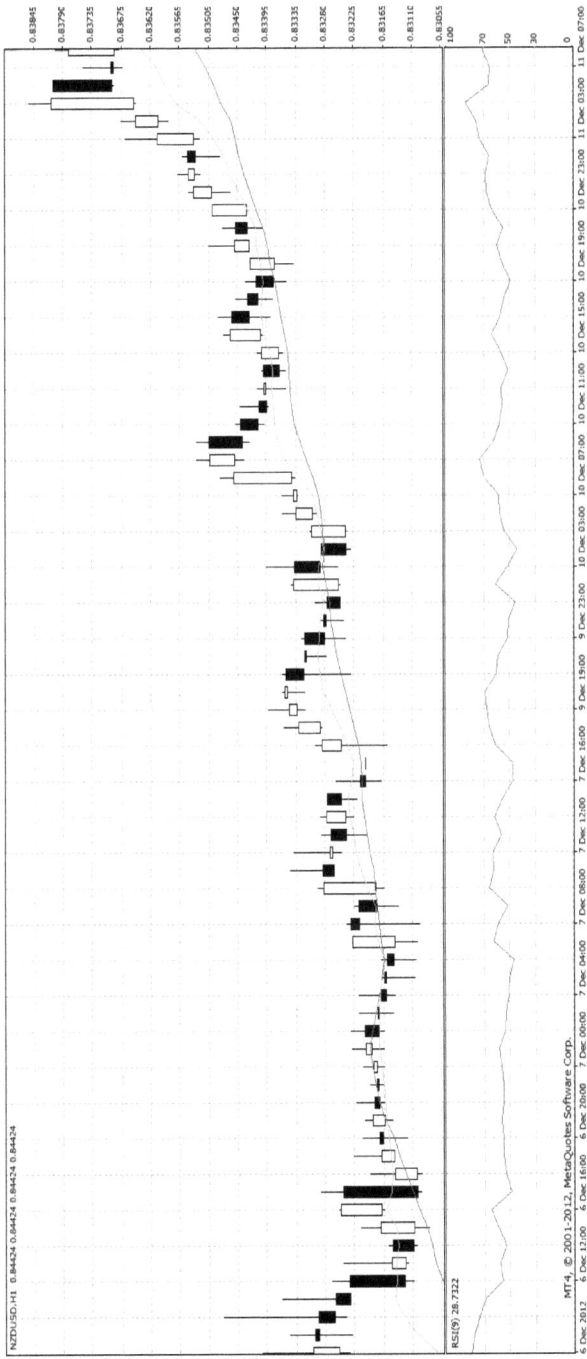

Figure 6.13: December 11, 2012 at 07:00

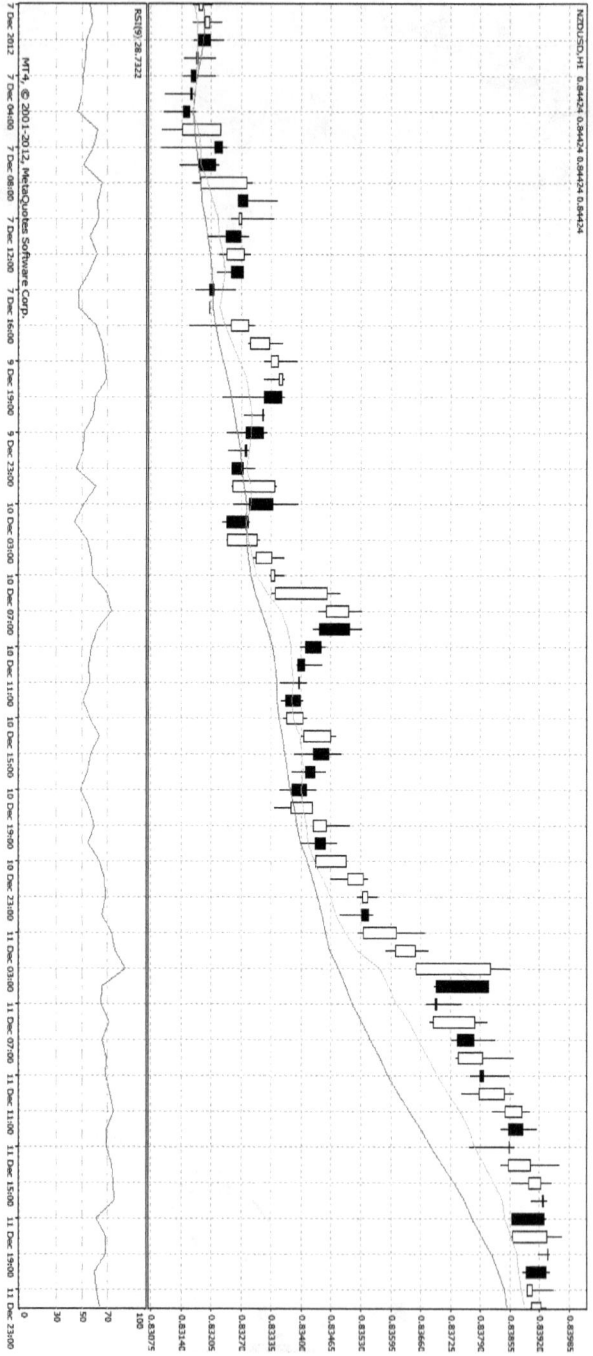

Figure 6.14: December 11, 2012 at 23:00

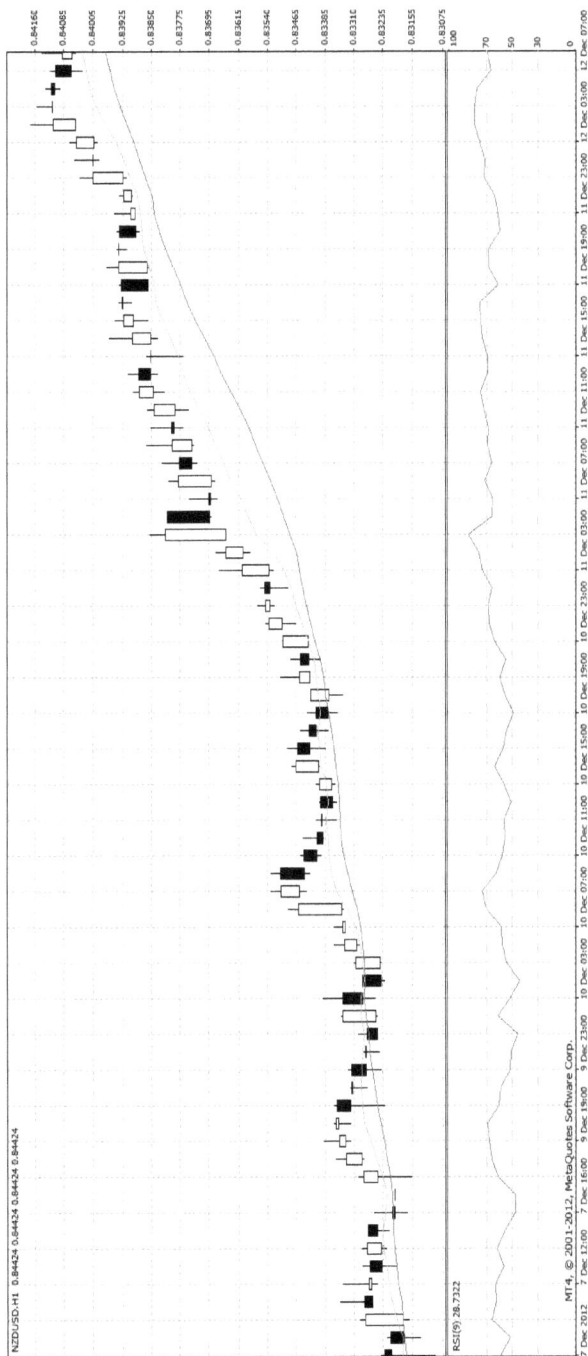

Figure 6.15: December 12, 2012 at 07:00

Figure 6.16: December 12, 2012 at 23:00

6.4.9 Day 9 - December 13, 2012

Bob continues his routine and wakes up at 07:00 and sees the same chart as Figure 6.17.

> "The chart continues to look clean. Still on an upward trend, so I'll see how things look at 12:00 when I have lunch."

At 12:00, Bob checks the chart again and sees something interesting. Figure 6.18 gives us the same view.

> "Well this is interesting. Looks like we're seeing some downwards pressure on the pair's price and this has triggered a crossover. Let me check my rules to see if I should switch positions:"
>
> - "EMA(11) is 0.84404 and SMA(19) is 0.84409, so the delta is just 0.5 pips. Not enough to trigger a trade."
> - "EMA(11) is lower than SMA(19), indicating a sell signal if the delta was larger."
> - "RSI(9) is 37.531."
>
> "RSI(9) has the right value for a *Sell* position, so there is possibility that this may be a legitimate reversal, but the moving average delta is too small. I'll check back in an hour."

At 13:00, Bob sees the chart as depicted by Figure 6.19.

> "Let me check the indicators again:"
>
> - "EMA(11) is 0.84380, SMA(19) is 0.84409. The moving average delta is 2.9 pips."

111

Figure 6.17: December 13, 2012 at 07:00

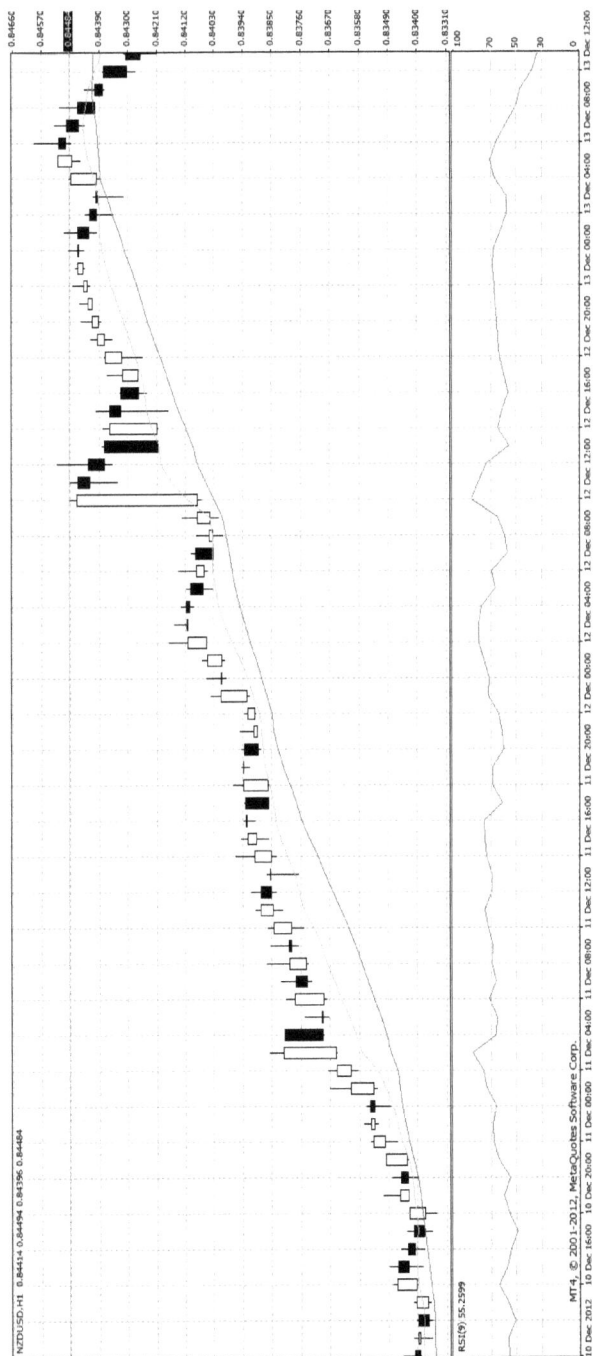

Figure 6.18: December 13, 2012 at 12:00

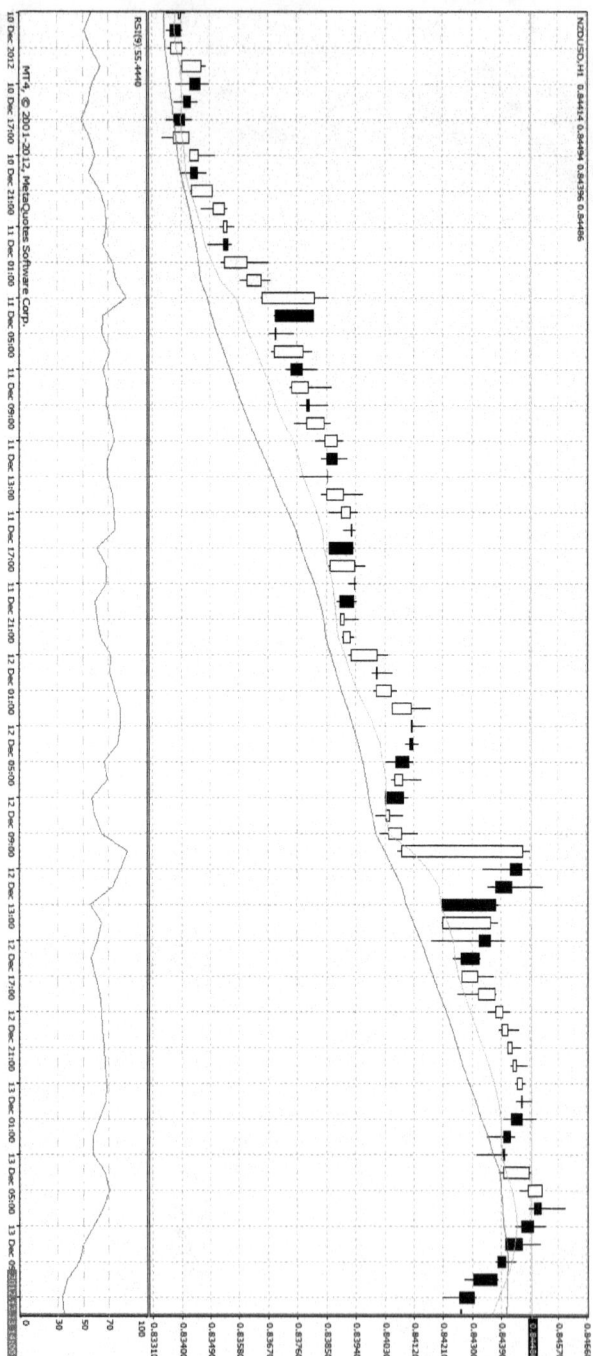

Figure 6.19: December 13, 2012 at 13:00

- "EMA(11) is lower than SMA(19), still indicating a sell signal."
- "RSI(9) is 33.134."

"Looks like the validity of this reversal is getting stronger. I'll check again in another hour."

Figure 6.20 shows what Bob found an hour later.

"It's 14:00 and it looks like the reversal can be confirmed. Time to check the indicators:"

- "EMA(11) is 0.84361, SMA(19) is 0.84406, giving a moving average delta of 4.5 pips."
- "EMA(11) is lower than SMA(19), still indicating a *Sell* signal."
- "RSI(9) is 34.289."

Bob closes out his order at 0.84252, giving him 214 pips of profit. That translates to $214 USD! Not bad for what essentially is a few hours of work, and by work I mean spending a few minutes checking out a chart every day for the past two weeks. Since the trend has reversed, Bob opens up a new *Sell* order. He opens his order at 0.84272 and sets his SL trigger at 0.84772 and his TP trigger at 0.81372.

At 23:00, Bob checks the chart and finds Figure 6.21 staring back at him. There seems to be a small pinch in the moving averages, but Bob is still happy with his earnings from earlier in the day so he pays it no heed.

"The rest of the day was uneventful. I notice that the price is rising as 23:00 comes closer, but I'm going to trust that things work out as I expect given how well this last trade worked! If this keeps up, I might just have to write a book about my trading prowess!"

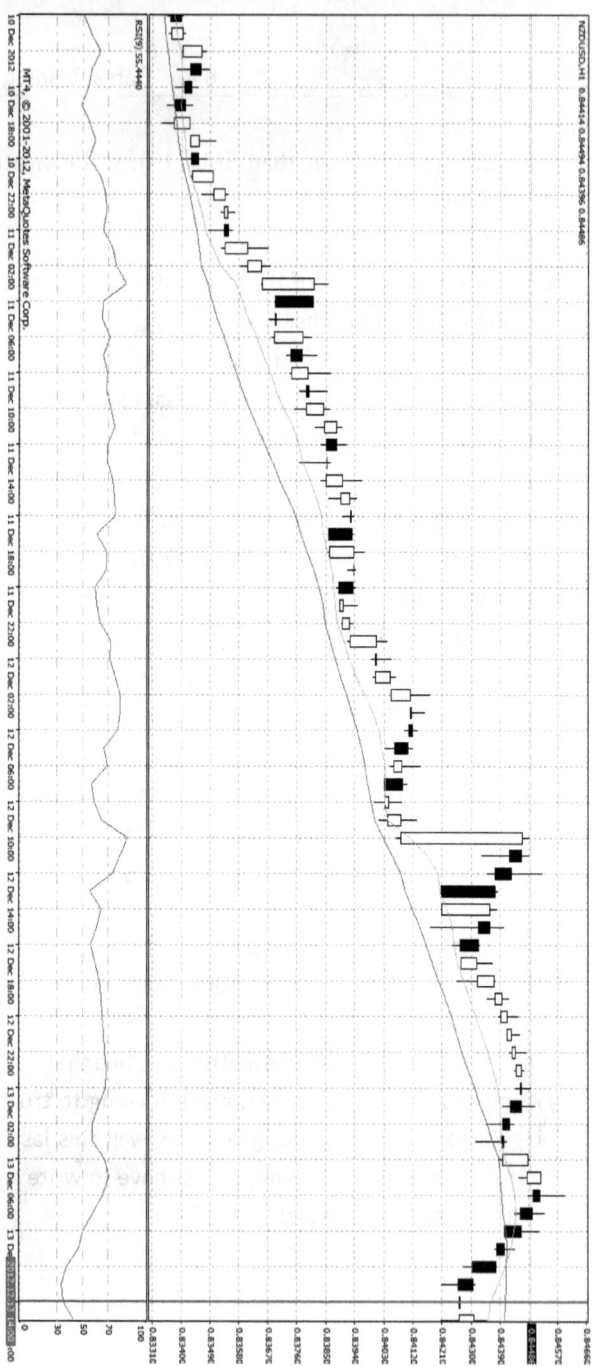

Figure 6.20: December 13, 2012 at 14:00

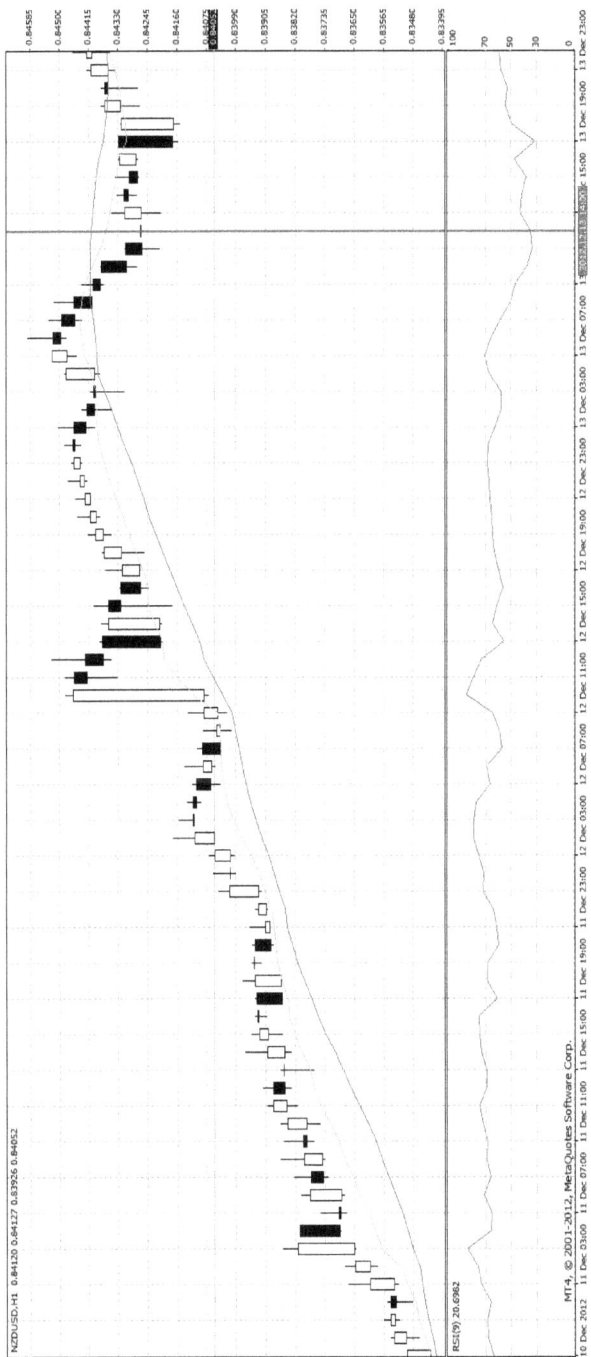

Figure 6.21: December 13, 2012 at 23:00

Oh Bob, 9 days does not make you an expert trader even if you did net a decent return.

6.4.10   Day 10 - December 14, 2012

At 07:00, Bob wakes and checks the chart. Figure 6.22 gives him a bit of a scare.

> "What happened?! It looks like there was a reversal around 02:00! A quick calculation shows that the moving average delta was 3.4 pips, so it did not fit in my rule set to trigger a reversal, but even if it did I would have slept right through it! I might have to watch the chart a little more often today."

What Bob experienced is not uncommon, and this is the risk of holding overnight positions if you cannot monitor them. Reversals can happen at any time, which is why it is **vital** to have a SL trigger in order to protect you.

At 12:00, Bob finds the same chart as Figure 6.23.

> "12:00. Seems like another reversal is happening, I'm going to continue to check this every hour on the hour."

Bob continues to watch the trends. At 15:00, he confirms the reversal.

> "Well it looks like it finally happened. Let me check the indicators and confirm:"

> - "EMA(11) is 0.84405, SMA(19) is 0.84329, giving a moving average delta of 7.6 pips."
> - "EMA(11) is higher than SMA(19), indicating a *Buy* signal."
> - "RSI(9) is 62.878."

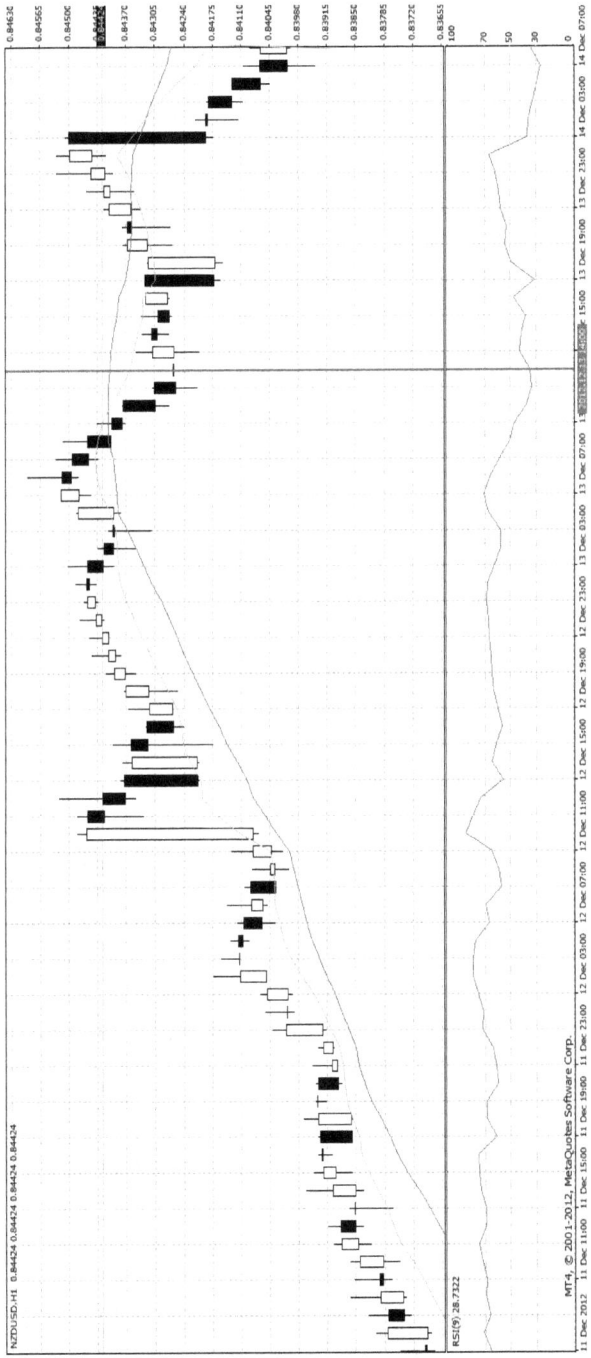

Figure 6.22: December 14, 2012 at 07:00

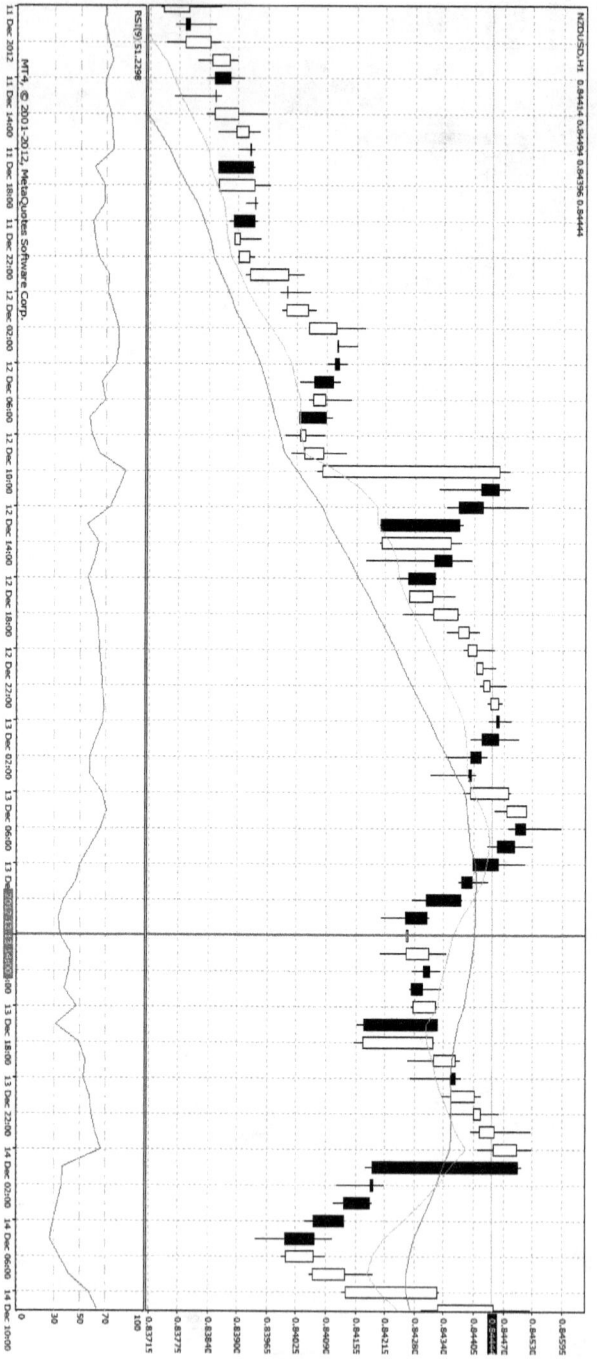

Figure 6.23: December 14, 2012 at 12:00

"Yes, that confirms it. It's time to switch positions."

Bob closes his existing order 0.84546. Since the order was originally opened at 0.84272, this gives Bob a net loss of $(0.84546 - 0.84272) \times 10000 = 27.4$ pips. He opens a new *Buy* order at 0.84566. Figure 6.24 depicts what the remainder of the day looked like. Since it is a Friday, the market closes at 17:00 and Bob calls it a week.

6.4.11 Day 11 - December 17, 2012

The weekend helped Bob put his recent loss into perspective:

> "After some rest and relaxation on the weekend, I came to grips with my loss. It was foolish to get that upset, especially since I had netted 214 pips of profit just the day before! So I lost just over 27 pips; I can deal with that."

At 07:00, Bob checked the chart and continues his daily routine. Figure 6.25 is what he finds.

> "What the?! Is this yet another reversal?! I better check the indicators:"

> - "EMA(11) is 0.84417, SMA(19) is 0.84480, giving a moving average delta of 6.3 pips."
> - "EMA(11) is lower than SMA(19), indicating a *Sell* signal."
> - "RSI(9) is 44.885."

The reversal is legitimate according to the trading rules we have outlined. Bob quickly close out his order at 0.84372 and nets a loss of 19.4 pips. Bob opens up a new *Sell* order at 0.84392 and makes himself a promise.

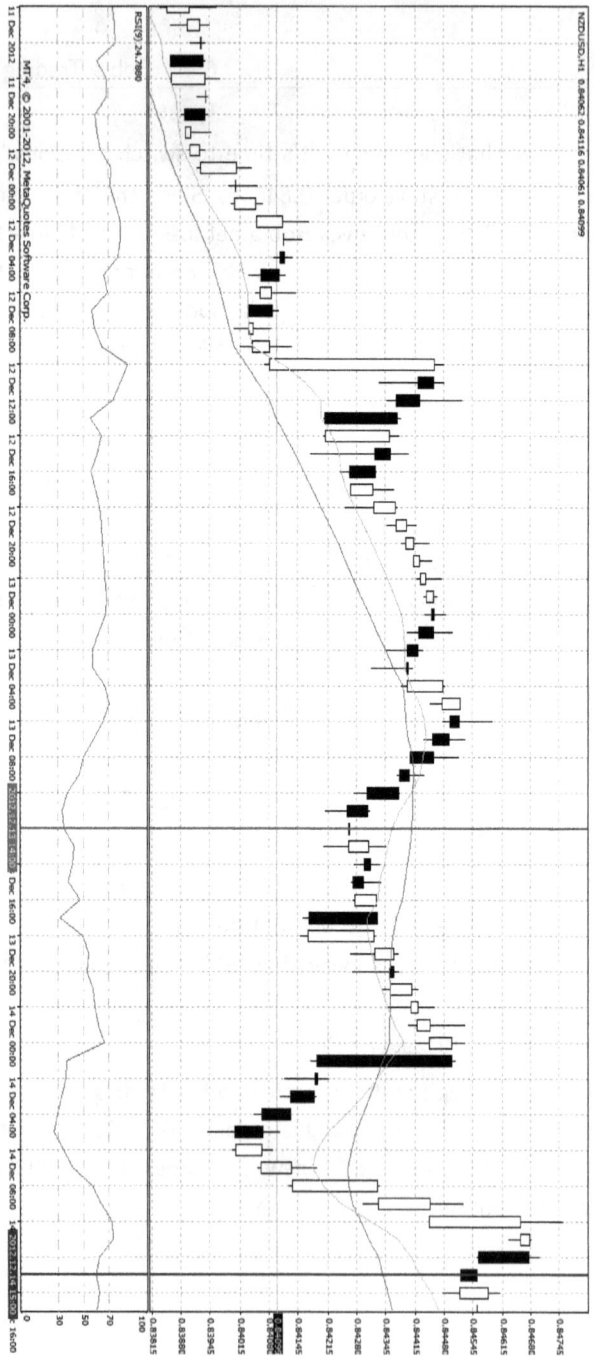

Figure 6.24: December 14, 2012 at 17:00

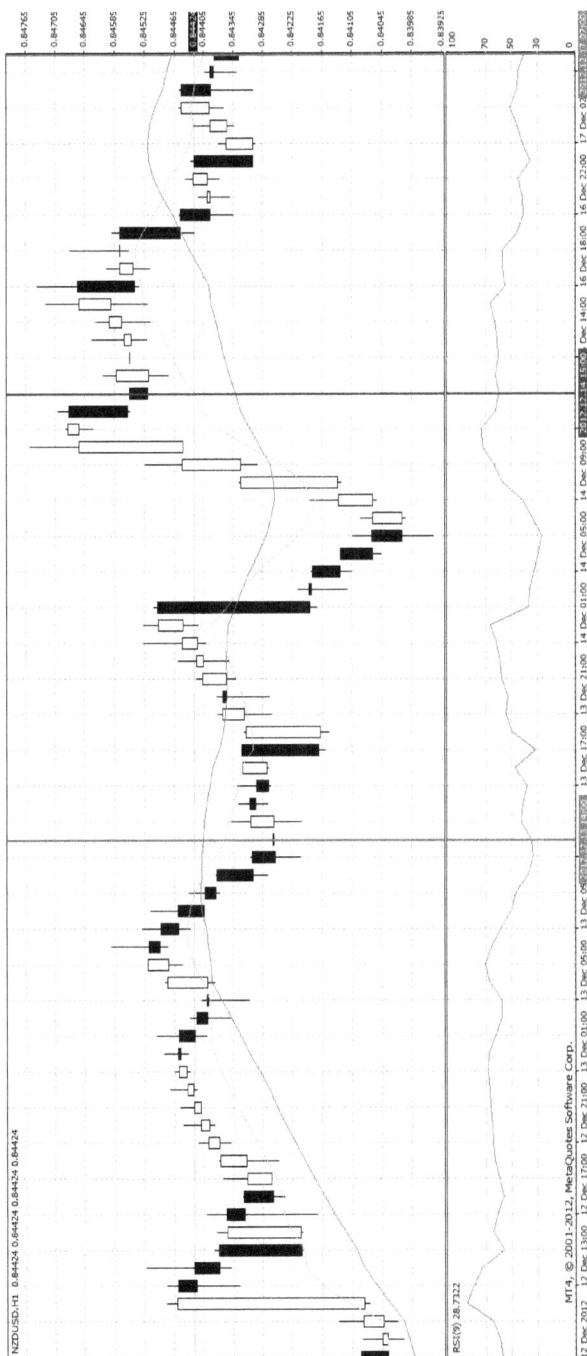

Figure 6.25: December 17, 2012 at 07:00

"I may still be in the black, but I was a fool for placing a new trade at the end of Friday. At the very least I should have monitored the price when it re-opened on Sunday! Oh well, at least I caught it early. I vow to be more cautious this time around."

The remainder of the day was uneventful. In fact starting at 14:00 right up to 23:00 when Bob heads off to bed the price for NZD/USD seems to have gone sideways, meaning that there was no real movement either way to cause Bob any concern. Figure 6.26 is the end-of-day chart that Bob reviews.

"There was a bit of sideways activity in the pair's price from 14:00 through to 23:00 today, but nothing to seriously worry about. I still have my SL trigger set and the trend seems to be continuing. I'll keep my fingers crossed as I sleep and check as soon as I wake up. I have a new app on my phone that lets me check my trade as soon as I wake up, so if I see a trend reversal, I can act on it that much faster[7]."

6.4.12   Day 12 - December 18, 2012

Figure 6.27 is the H1 chart Bob sees at 07:00. It seems that the downward trend is continuing, meaning his *Sell* order is continuing nicely.

The remainder of the day is uneventful. Bob checks the chart every few hours while at work and also when he gets home. No indications

---

[7]Do not become obsessed with watching your orders. This introduces unwanted emotion, paranoia and ultimately losses. If you have such an app, use it sparingly.

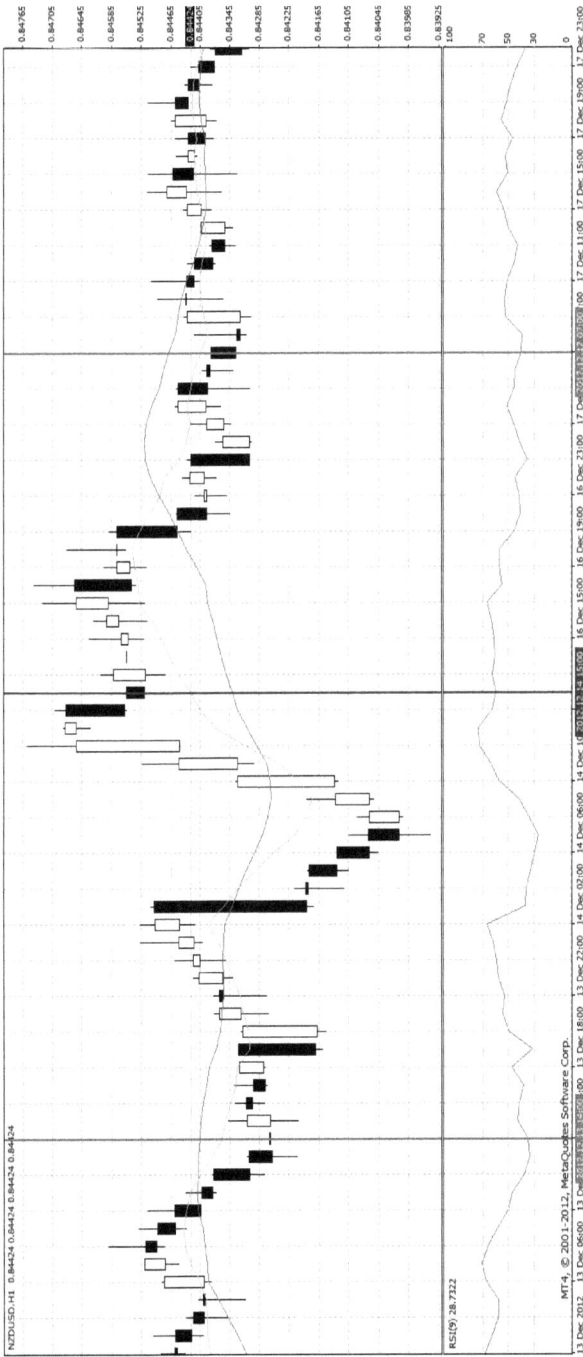

Figure 6.26: December 17, 2012 at 23:00

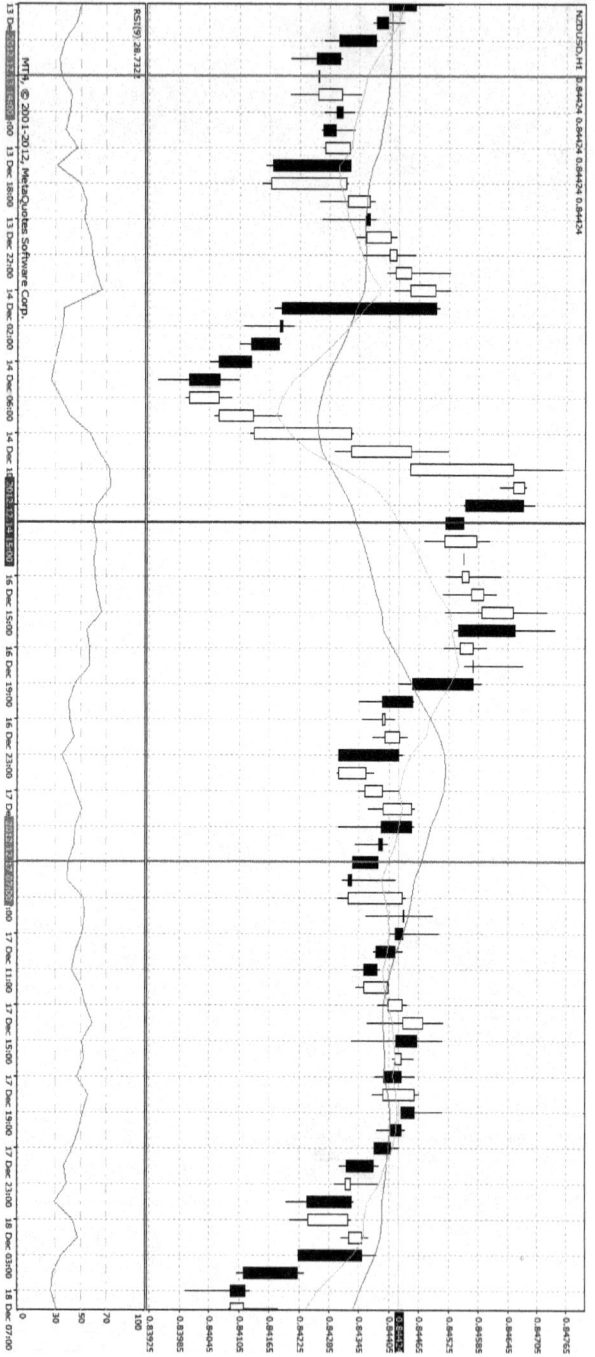

Figure 6.27: December 18, 2012 at 07:00

that he needs to act, so he heads off to bed for the night. Figure 6.28 shows the chart for the remainder of the day right up to 23:00.

6.4.13 Day 13 - December 19, 2012

Lucky day 13! Bob wakes up and checks the chart as seen in Figure 6.29

> "The morning check is again showing a good trend. No reason to panic today. I'll check the chart throughout the day."

The trend continues without fail for the remainder of the day. Figure 6.30 shows the chart at 23:00, which is the last chart Bob checks for the day.

6.4.14 Day 14 - December 20, 2012

At 07:00, Bob wakes up and looks at the chart depicted by Figure 6.31.

> "There was some minor activity overnight, but nothing strong enough to break the trend. I'll check during my coffee breaks just to make sure nothing sneaks up on me."

Bob monitors the H1 chart throughout the day, but by 23:00 he sees no changes to the trend, so he heads off to bed. Figure 6.32 is the last chart he reviews for the day.

6.4.15 Day 15 - December 21, 2012

> "Friday. Another consolidation day perhaps? If it is, I won't make the same mistake again and open a new order

Figure 6.28: December 18, 2012 at 23:00

Figure 6.29: December 19, 2012 at 07:00

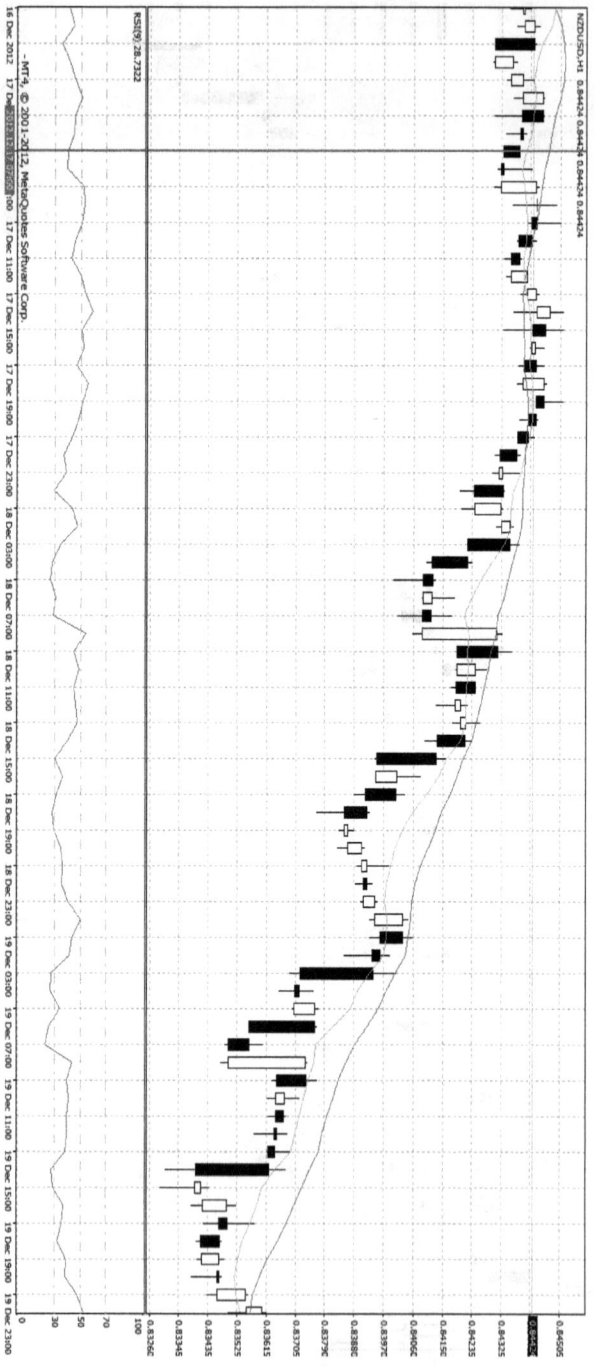

Figure 6.30: December 19, 2012 at 23:00

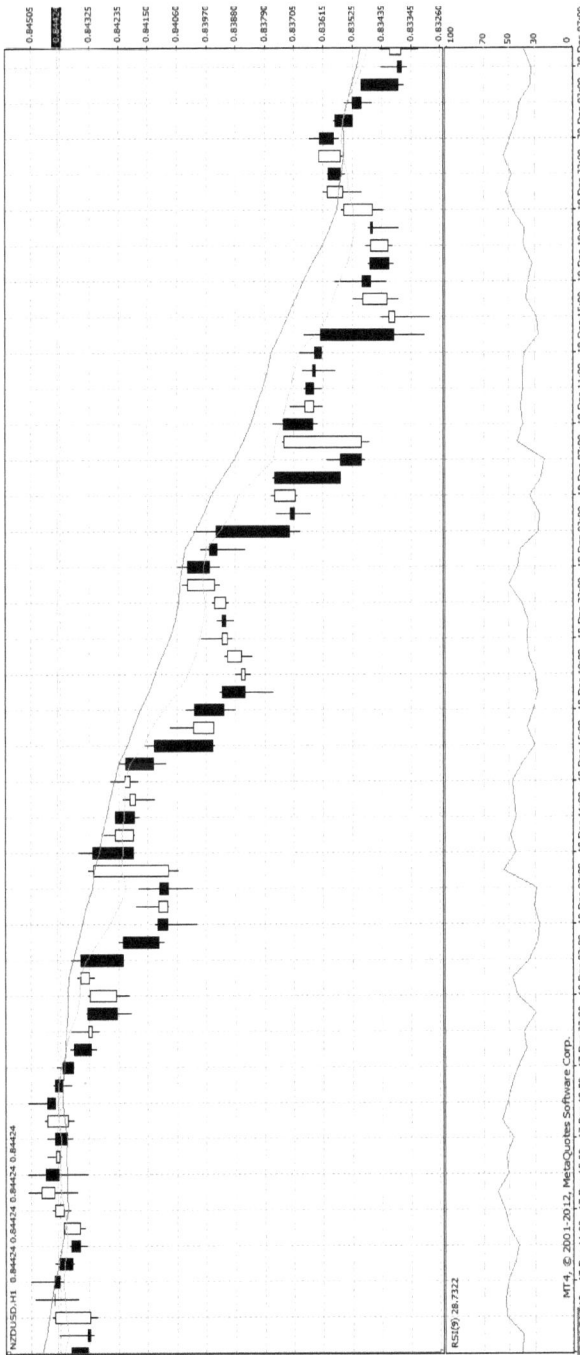

Figure 6.31: December 20, 2012 at 07:00

Figure 6.32: December 20, 2012 at 23:00

right at the end of the day! That was foolish considering
I don't watch the market on Sunday."

Looking at the first chart of the day at 07:00, Bob reviews the same
activity as seen in Figure 6.33.

"The overnight chart looks clean. It might be a quiet day
after all."

Bob heads to work and puts in a full day. He monitors the chart a
few times during the day but he doesn't see any reversals pending. At
17:00, he checks the final chart of the week as seen in Figure 6.34.

"No change in the trend. RSI(9) looks interesting, but
it doesn't give me any reason to change my position. I
suppose this is why it is best to use multiple indicators to
make sure that you don't rush into things. I wonder how
next week will look."

With that, Bob heads home for the day and begins to enjoy his weekend.

6.4.16   Day 16 - December 24, 2012

In the final week of trading for this exercise, Bob wakes up at 07:00
and faces the chart that we see in Figure 6.35.

"The chart seems to indicate a sideways trend, so I'll just
have to keep an eye out throughout the day to see if anything happens. The markets will be closing early today
given that it's Christmas eve and all, so it should make
for a nice short day."

As the markets close for Christmas at 12:00, Bob takes one last look
and sees no change as we ourselves can see in Figure 6.36.

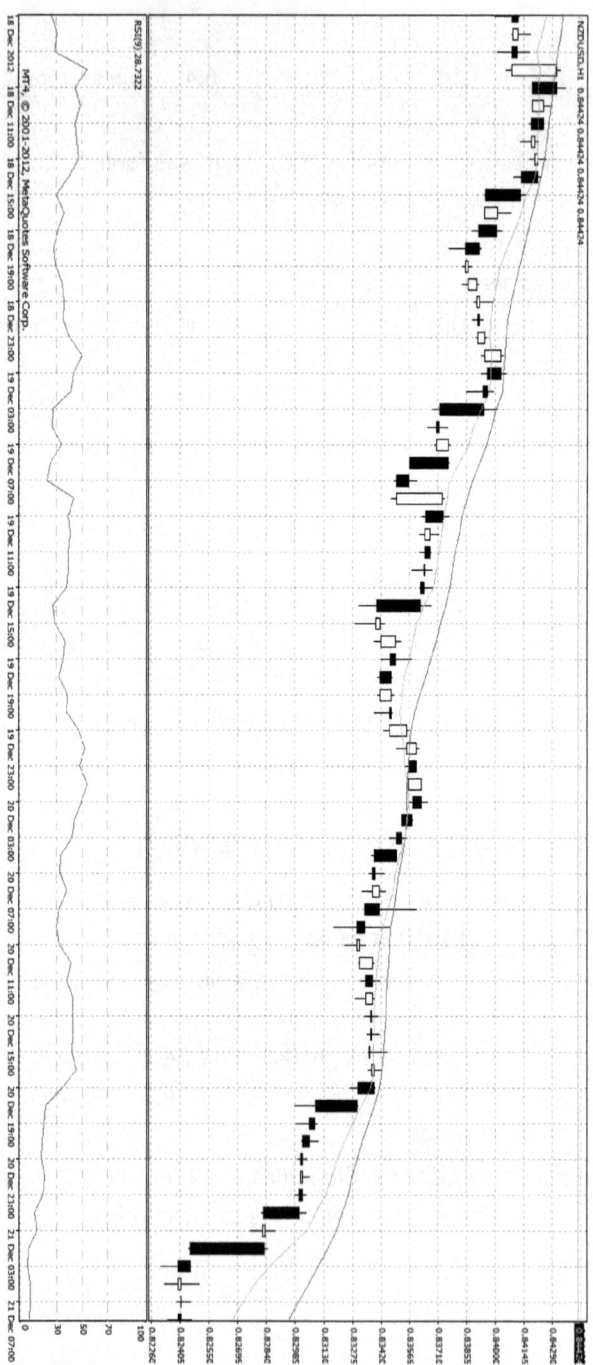

Figure 6.33: December 21, 2012 at 07:00

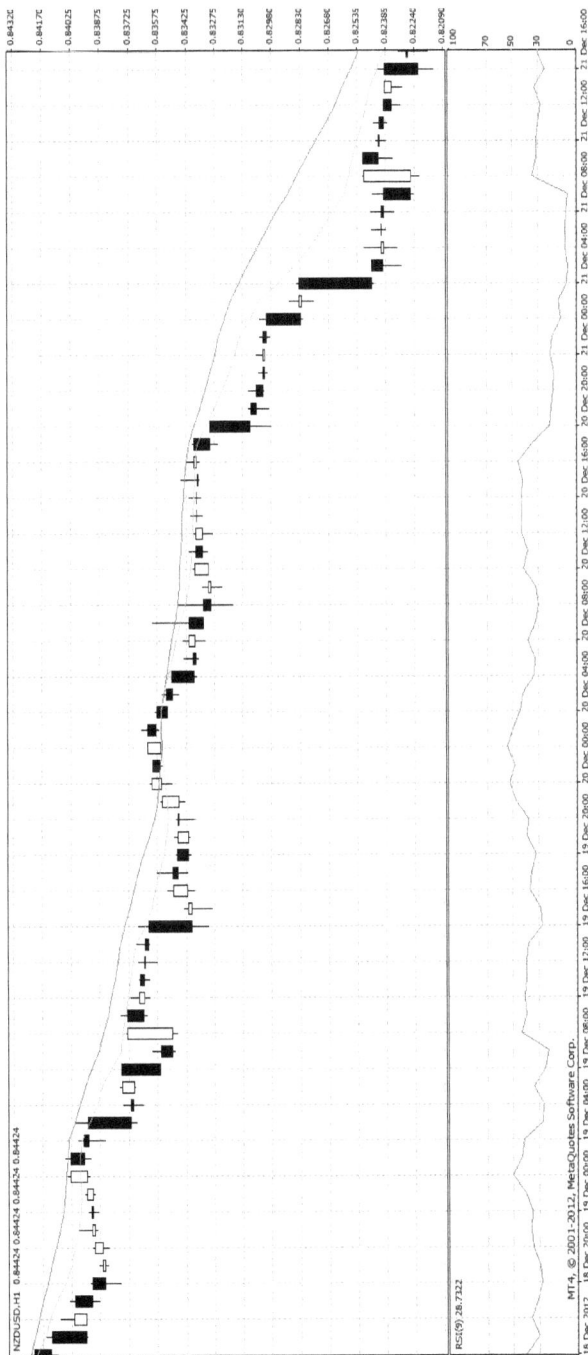

Figure 6.34: December 21, 2012 at 17:00

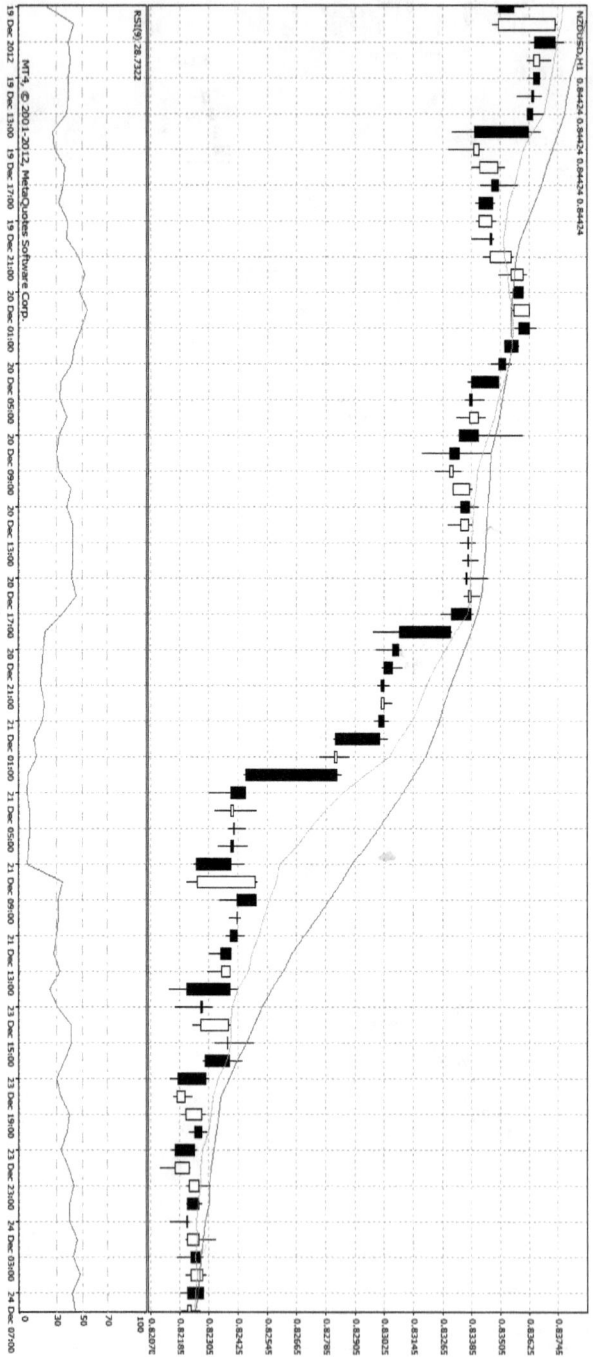

Figure 6.35: December 24, 2012 at 07:00

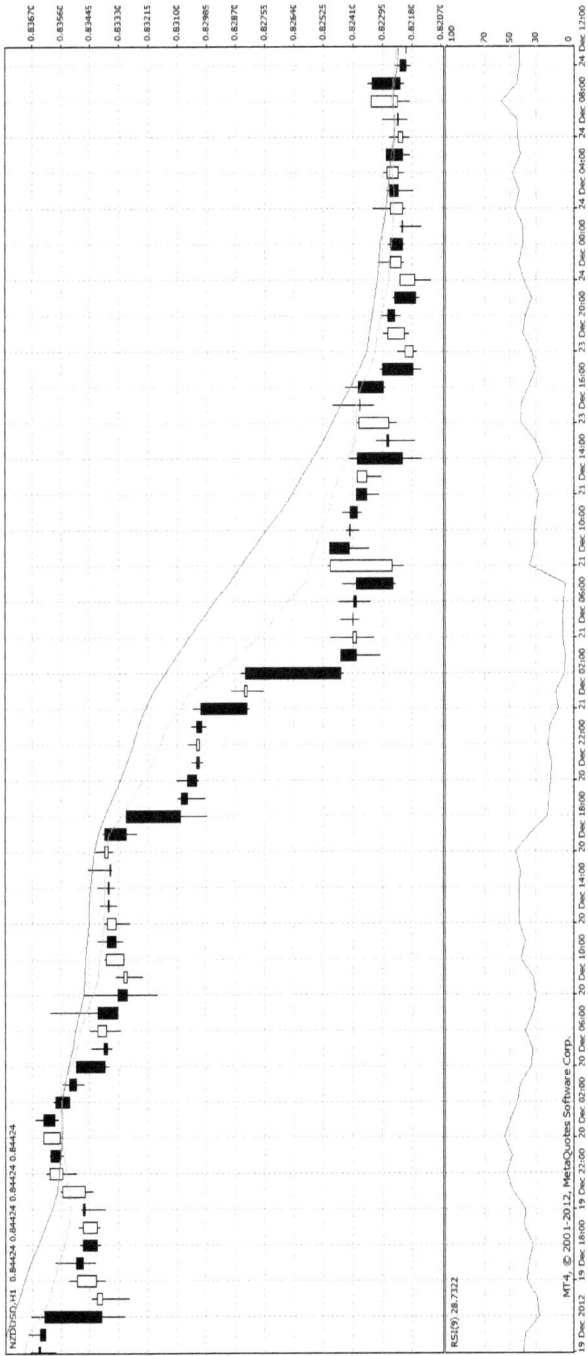

Figure 6.36: December 24, 2012 at 12:00

6.4.17 Day 17 - December 26, 2012

With the markets closed for Christmas day, Bob awakes on the 26th and checks the chart at 07:00. Figure 6.37 is what he sees.

> "Wow! What a drop! I think the markets may have given me yet another Christmas present!"

The drop in price strengthens Bob's *Sell* order, making him a happy camper. Bob heads to work and checks every few hours before returning home. At 23:00 he checks the H1 chart again, as depicted in Figure 6.38.

> "Looks like the market is going sideways a bit tonight. I'm still in good profit territory, so I'm not too concerned. There is a bit of a crossover forming at 23:00, but I'm tired and I've seen this type of movement before. I'm not sure that anything is going to change drastically, so I'm willing to let the market do what it wants as I get some sleep."

6.4.18 Day 18 - December 27, 2012

At 07:00, Bob looks at the chart and sees something interesting as we ourselves can see in Figure 6.39.

> "Looks like we have a reversal! Time to check the indicators. I'm currently making a good profit on this trade, so it wouldn't hurt me to close out now. Still, I want to double-check the indicators and check my rules before I do anything. Let me check the indicators:"
>
> - "EMA(11) is 0.82038, SMA(19) is 0.81961, giving a moving average delta of 7.7 pips."

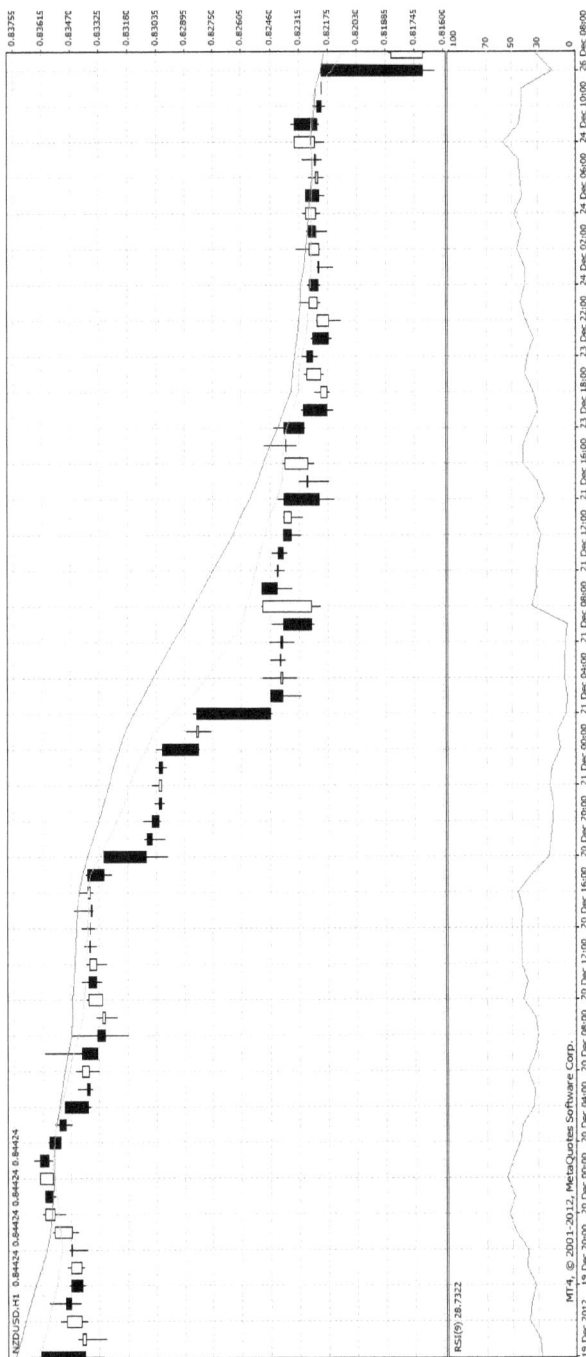

Figure 6.37: December 26, 2012 at 07:00

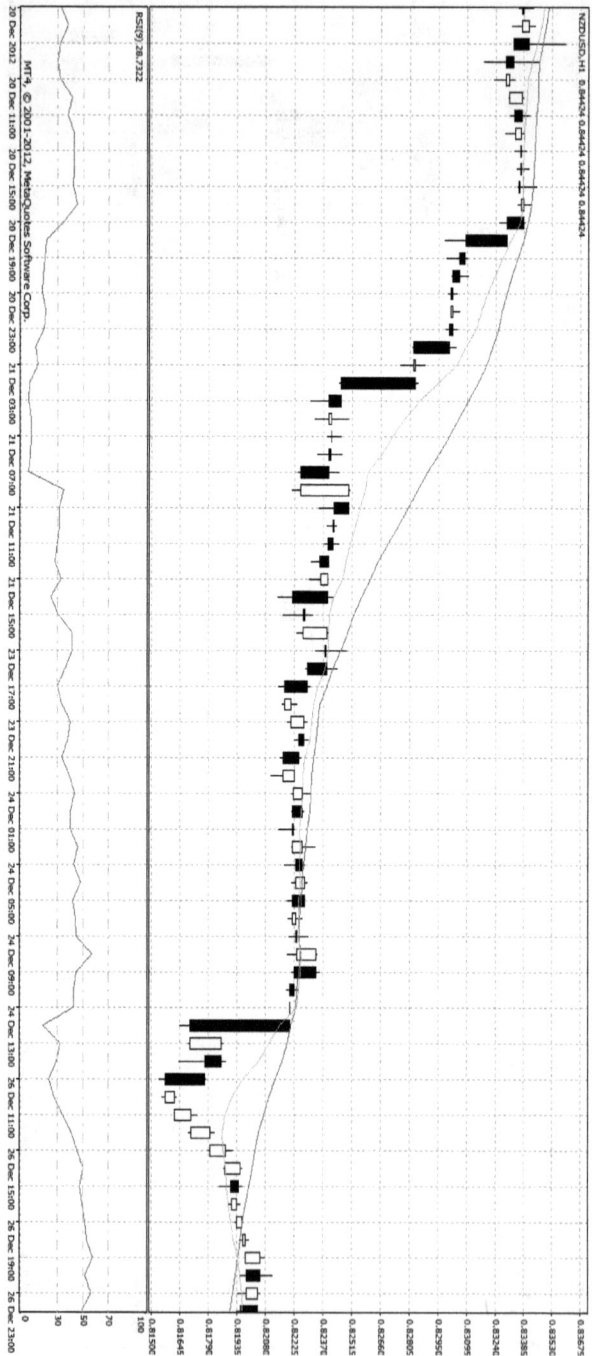

Figure 6.38: December 26, 2012 at 23:00

Figure 6.39: December 27, 2012 at 07:00

- "EMA(11) is higher than SMA(19), indicating a *Buy* signal."
- "RSI(9) is sitting 49.867, which is just below 50."

Bob isn't sure what to make of this. So far two of his three indicators are showing that there is a reversal, yet RSI(9) hasn't confirmed this even though it is close. Bob decides to head into the office and check in a few hours to see what happens. He's still making a profit with this trade, so he's not willing to close it out just yet. This is a hard decision, and closing out now and reversing wouldn't necessarily be seen as the wrong move, but he wants to stick to his trading rules and he decides to wait.

At 12:00, Bob sees the same chart as Figure 6.40.

> "Looks like the trend did continue after all. Great news! That was close though, so I'm wondering if the pair is preparing for a trend reversal."

Bob continues his day, monitoring the price movement every few hours. He continued to monitor after he gets home. As we can see in Figure 6.41, a crossover occurs around 18:00. Bob continues to monitor the crossover hourly up until 23:00, when he checks the indicators again.

> "It seems that the crossover has hit critical mass. Time for another rule check:"

- "EMA(11) is 0.82021, SMA(19) is 0.81967, giving a moving average delta of 5.4 pips."
- "EMA(11) is higher than SMA(19), indicating a *Buy* signal."
- "RSI(9) is 63.089, giving another *Buy* signal."

142

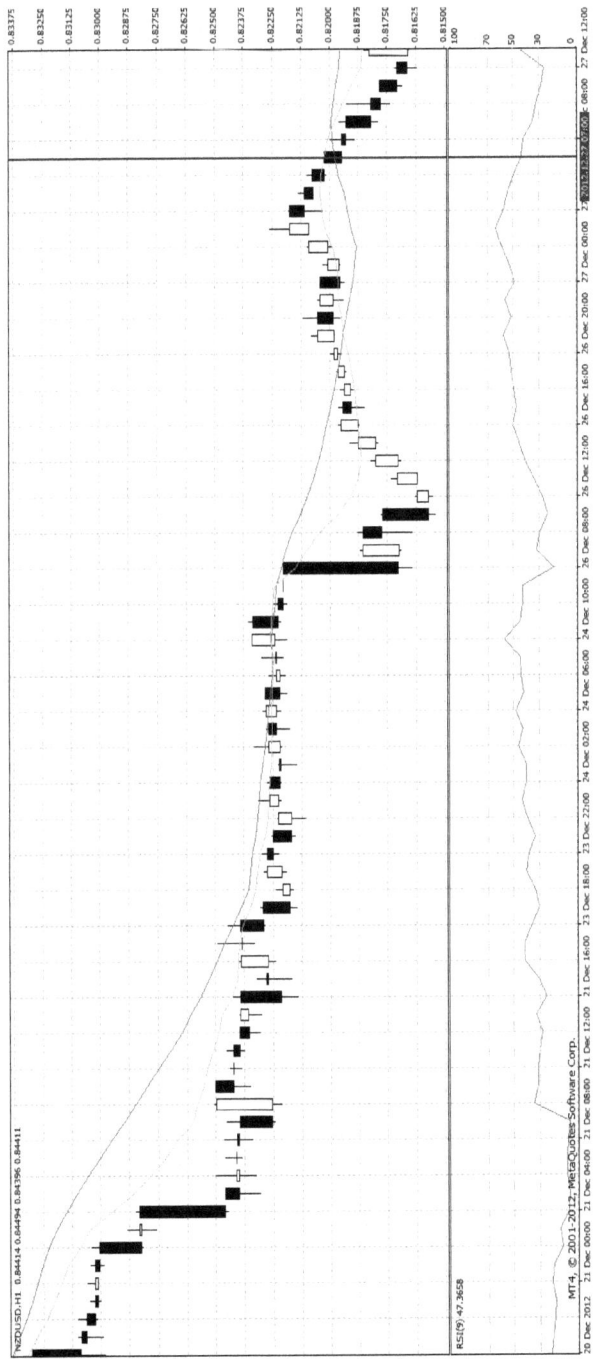

Figure 6.40: December 27, 2012 at 12:00

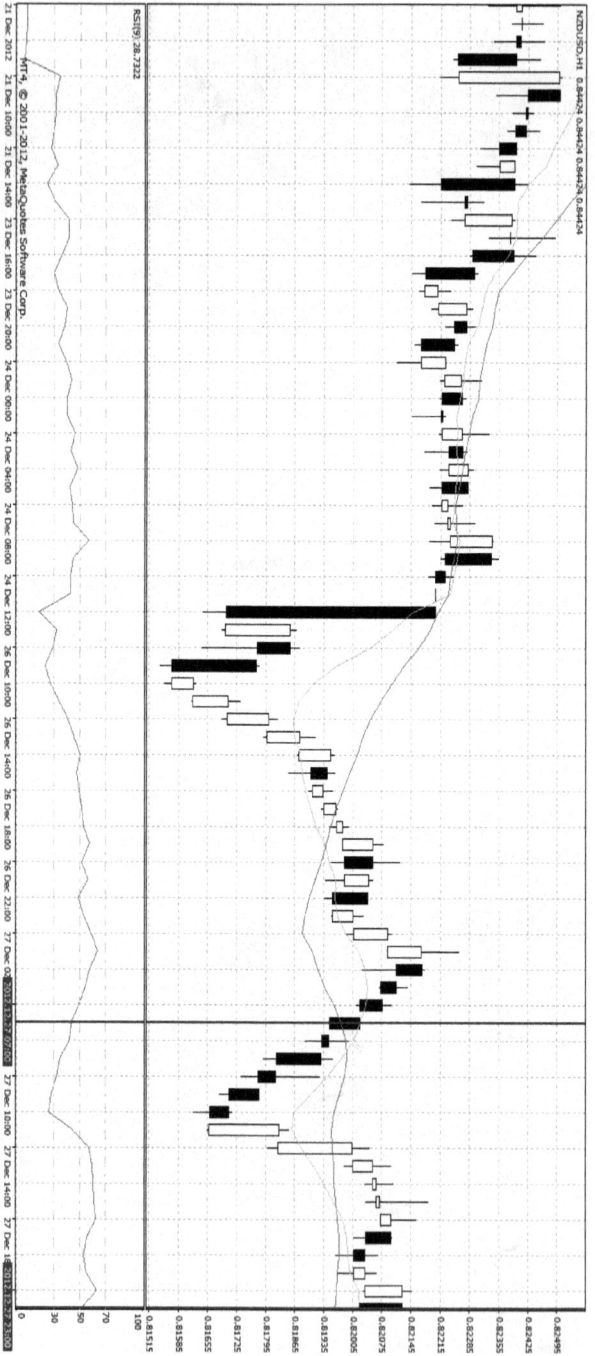

Figure 6.41: December 27, 2012 at 23:00

Bob closes out his *Sell* order at 0.82115 and nets himself a nice 220 pip profit. He then opens up a new *Buy* order at 0.82135, hopeful that he can squeeze in a few more pips before the end of the year.

6.4.19 Day 19 - December 28, 2012

With only two days to go, Bob continues to watch the market with great interest and enthusiasm. Figure 6.42 shows the market at 07:00.

> "The market seems quiet today, but this makes sense. New years day is coming up, so I don't expect a lot of activity from traders."

Bob continues to monitor every few hours as he has become accustomed to doing, but aside from a small crossover in the early afternoon there were no crossovers worth examining. Figure 6.43 shows the price movement up to 23:00, at which point Bob decides to call it a day and goes off to bed.

6.4.20 Day 20 - December 31, 2012

Bob wakes up and prepares for another short trading day. Today is the last day of his 20 days of trading and so he begins the same way as he has for the past few weeks, by looking at the H1 chart for NZD/USD. Figure 6.44 is what he sees.

> "All is still quiet in the Forex today. I suppose that most traders are taking time off between Christmas and New Year's. Makes sense, and the market shows it. The market will close at 12:00 today due to the holiday, so at least it will be a short day."

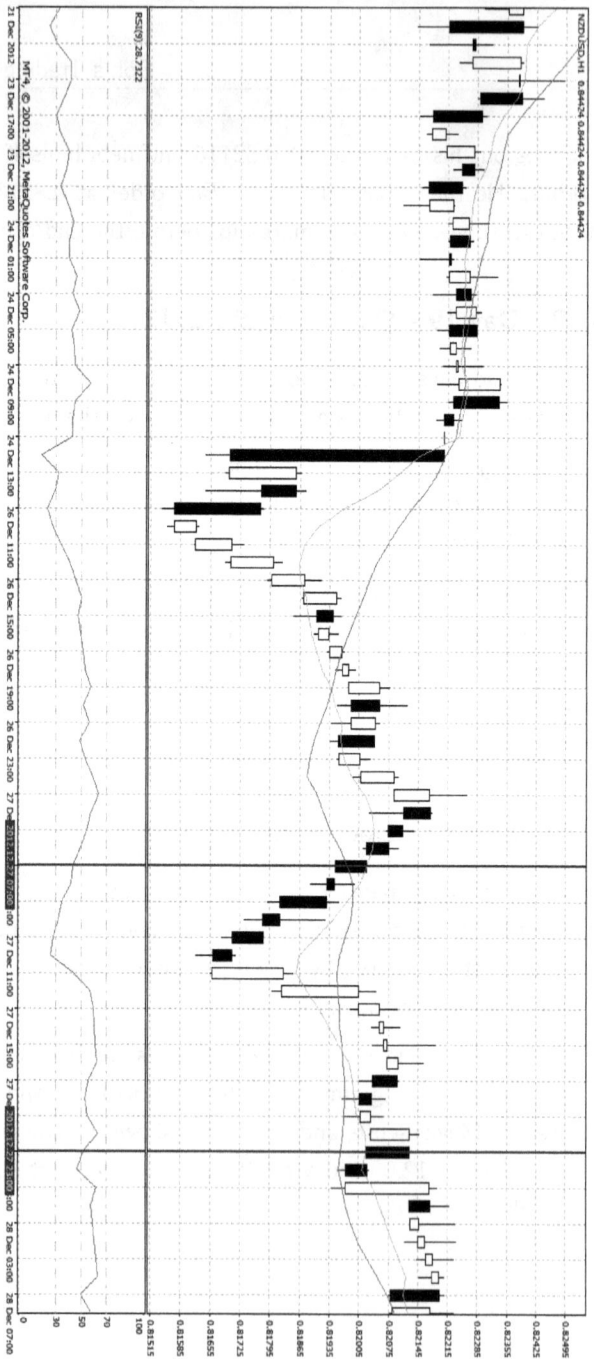

Figure 6.42: December 28, 2012 at 07:00

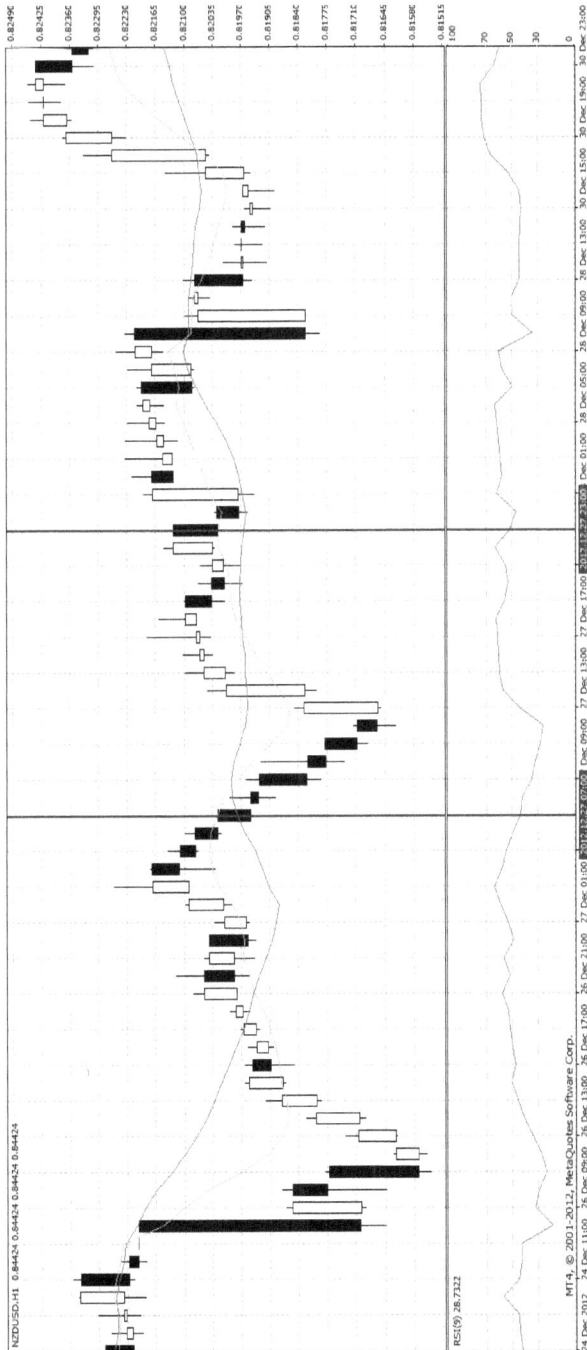

Figure 6.43: December 28, 2012 at 23:00

Figure 6.44: December 31, 2012 at 07:00

At 12:00, Bob checks the chart for the last time and sees that nothing has changed. Figure 6.45 shows what the final price movement looked like for Bob.

Bob closes out his last trade at 0.82643, giving him a profit of 50.8 pips. Not bad, not bad at all. So for all of December Bob managed to net 438 pips of profit, or $438 USD. For all the checking he did, he really didn't spend that much time monitoring the charts each day. Overall, Bob is quite satisfied with his Forex trading, and plans on continuing with the same rule set in the near future.

6.5 Summary

That wraps up Bob's trading adventure. I hope you found it insightful and fun to read. Trading the Forex may seem daunting to newcomers, but in reality by using the right tools, laying out some simple rules and **following** those rules anyone can start trading the Forex and make a profit.

There are a few things that Bob learned during his 20 days of trading:

1. Not all orders will close the same day they are opened.

2. Having a clear set of rules for your trades will help you immensely.

3. Losses are inevitable, so when they happen try not to let them bother you.

Part of Bob's success is in using a longer time period when plotting the NZD/USD prices. New traders want to use smaller time periods since it is easier to make trades and see instant results. Please resist this urge since it will lead you down the path of great losses. New

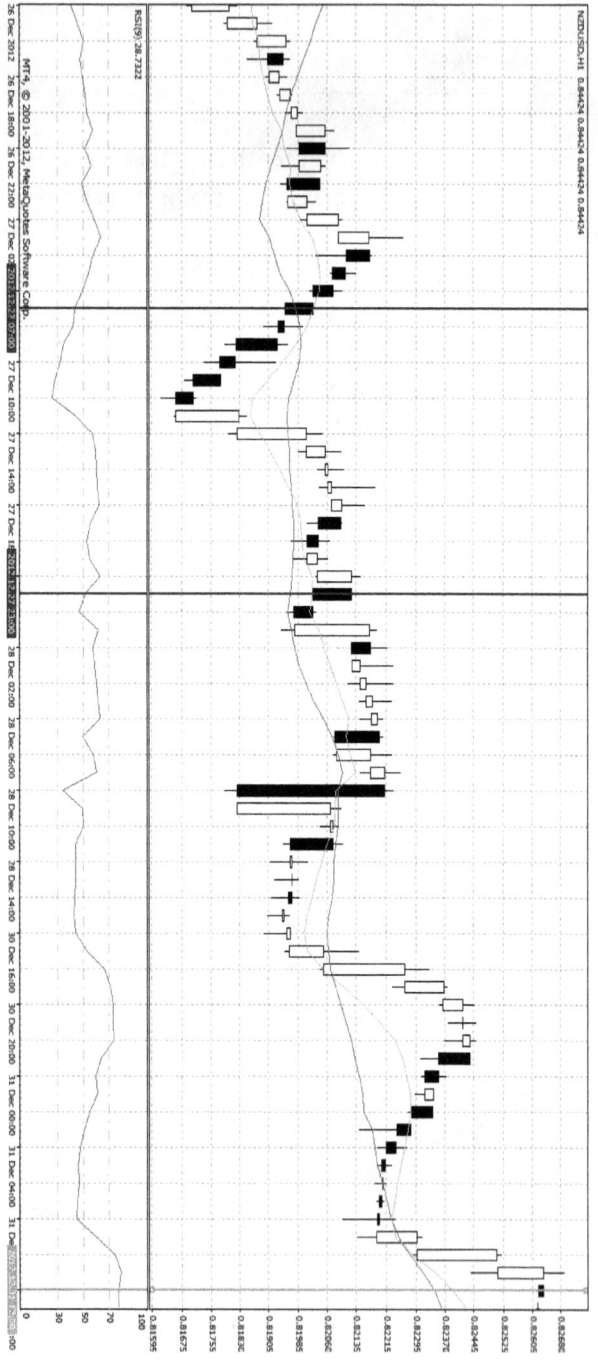

Figure 6.45: December 31, 2012 at 12:00

traders should stick to the H1 and even H4 charts and look for clear trends before making any kind of trade. Until you are comfortable with a set of rules and a trading methodology that works for you, I would strongly recommend staying away from the smaller time periods.

A strong set of rules in place will help make your trading experience smoother. Having a strict set of rules to follow gives you something to stick to in times of uncertainty as well as a starting point for automating your trading.

Finally you need to accept that you will have losing trades. Accept it, embrace it, and try to separate your emotions from it. If you have a money management plan in place, such as the 2% rule, then you do not need to worry about losing your fortune. Also remember to never trade without a stop loss trigger in place. Remember, triggers will protect you as you sleep.

I strongly encourage you to go out and open a practice account and trade to your heart's content. Do not use real money until you have *at least* 3 - 6 *months* of practice account trading experience under your belt. There is a huge difference between practice and live accounts, so the more experience you have executing on proven strategies, the better. Practice is one thing that I feel most Forex books do not stress enough. Without practice, emotions will kick in and you will start to doubt your set of trading rules. When doubt creeps in, that's when losses start to grow. For what it's worth, I still use my practice account to this day to ensure any new strategies I try to execute on will actually work before I put them to use on my live account. Practice never hurts!

In the next chapter I want to share with you some other investment options other than Forex that you might want to consider for growing your money tree. Remember, a tree needs more than just sunlight to grow.

CHAPTER 7

Diversify, Diversify, Diversify!

In farming, there is the concept of *crop rotation*, which is where farmers plant different crops in the same field in subsequent seasons. The reason they do this is to benefit the soil by ensuring the nitrogen levels are improved, the risk of parasites for a particular crop building up is diminished, as well as a variety of other benefits. I'm not a farmer, but I am a fan of their ideas.

Often times when someone begins to take control of their personal finances, the first thing they do is read a book on the subject. These books may cover stocks, Forex, bonds, futures, real estate, or a variety of other topics. After reading such a book, people tend to believe that what they just read is the *only* thing they need to do in order to "strike it rich"!

Realistically there is no single "ultimate" investment option available. If there were, then every major bank and billionaire in the world would use that single option. Of course this is not the case, so what do they actually do?

Banks and other large investment groups *diversify* their investments; they invest in different things to make sure that they don't keep "all their eggs in one basket". While some people can make a killing doing just one thing, the reality is that it can be a lot less stressful to spread your investments around. If one of your investments goes bad, you don't lose all your money with it.

In this chapter I will cover some different ways to diversify your investments and help your money tree grow safely by avoiding the "all your eggs in one basket" trap.

7.1 Traditional Investments

When I talk about *traditional investments*, I am talking about things like *Guaranteed Investment Certificates (GICs)*, *mutual funds*, *savings bonds* and other investment options often offered by your bank, credit union, or financial planner. These investment choices are mostly aimed at people who have a low-to-medium appetite for risk; people who prefer financial stability and comfort in exchange for a smaller return on their investments.

Is there anything wrong with this approach? Absolutely not! I just wouldn't put *all* my money in these investment options. Why not? Well, some of these options require you to "lock" your money in the investment for some period of time. This can be as short as 3 months, but can range up to 5 year commitment. Let me give my views on some different investment options available[1] to help grow your own money tree.

---

[1] I am going to be covering Canadian specific investment options, but most countries offer similar options.

Remember, no one has a more vested interest in your financial future than you do! Always do your own due-diligence and research all available options when deciding on what type of investment options you want to use to grow your own money tree. Diversification is important, but blindly putting your money into an investment option without understanding it can be just as detrimental to your money tree's health as not diversifying at all.

7.2 Savings Bonds

A *Savings Bond* is usually offered either at the provincial or federal level. When you purchase a bond, you are in essence investing in the province or country, depending on which you choose[2]! Since a country is not likely to go bankrupt anytime in the foreseeable future, something like a Canada savings bond is a good low-risk choice. Savings bonds generally have a low rate of returns and fairly long periods before they reach their maximum value. You can, however, cash out savings bonds at any time at any major bank. Interest will be paid up to the last full month of the bond, so it certainly helps to hold the bond for as long as possible in order to maximize your return on investment.

The one downside to cashing out a savings bond before it's maturity date is that you do not get the full interest payment you would have received had you waited. At the time of this writing, the annual interest rate for a regular interest rate Canada savings bond held for

---

[2]Savings bonds are not the same as the bonds purchased on the *bond market*. I will not be covering those in this book.

3 years is 1.0% for the first year, 1.2% for the second year and 1.4% for the third year. Not a spectacular growth, but an incredibly stable one and definitely better than what you would be making if you kept your money in just a standard checking or savings account.

However savings bonds come with a catch - you can only purchase them at specific times during the year. Canada savings bonds are generally only available for purchase from early October through to the beginning of December. You also must purchase the bonds in specific denominations, ranging from $100 to $10,000.

Bonds are a great way to get a small return with very little risk. Given their flexibly by being able to cash a savings bond out at any time, they are a great low-risk choice to grow your money tree if you want something better than a low-to-no interest checking or savings account.

7.3 Guaranteed Investment Certificate (GIC)

Banks, trusts and credit unions offer an investment choice known as a *Guaranteed Investment Certificate*, or *GIC* for short. These are fixed term investments, with the term ranging from 3 months to 5 years and (as the name implies) offers a guaranteed rate of return for the investment. There are only two ways you will not receive the posted rate of return for your investment:

1. If the bank, trust or credit union defaults.

2. If you withdraw your money before the end of the term[3]

The first case is not likely, especially if you are dealing with a bank that is registered with the Canadian Deposit Insurance Corporation

---

[3]This is for a *non-cashable* or *closed* GIC.

(CDIC)[4]. The risk of a bank defaulting on a GIC is pretty slim, so it's highly unlikely that you would ever deal with the CDIC. Canadian banks are considered some of the safest and best managed banks in the world[5], so there is very little chance of any of them defaulting on anything they offer.

The second case, however, is something that not all new investors are aware of when they consider investing in a GIC. In addition to requiring a minimum amount to invest, you must keep your money in the GIC for the full term in order to be paid any interest if you are dealing with a *closed* GIC. If you try to cash out early, you will forfeit any interest you may have earned and there is a good chance you must also have to pay a penalty fee!

GICs are a great choice if you have a low appetite for risk, have some money lying around that you just want to grow slowly and not need for some time.

So Many GIC Options!

Banks normally offer two different "classes" of GIC; a *non-cashable* one that I have described previously and a *cashable* option. The *non-cashable* GIC will incur a penalty if closed before its term but tends to offers a higher interest rate. The *cashable* GIC allows you to cash out at any time without penalty, but offers a lower interest rate.

---

[4]The CDIC will cover up to $100,000 of your GIC as long as it has a maturity term of 5 years or less

[5]World Economic Forum Report, 2010-2011

GICs come in a variety of investment options. One popular option offers a *maximum* return, meaning that if the GIC exceeds the maximum then you do not get the share of the profits. The maximum is usually pretty high, usually a few percentage points above a non-maximum GIC, but there is no guarantee that the GIC will reach that maximum rate of return. If the maximum rate is exceeded, then you will be paid only up to that maximum percentage on your investment. Oh, and that maximum rate is for the initial investment. Basically that means if the maximum rate is 10% for a 5 year GIC, then if the GIC makes 12% in the first two years, you will only receive a maximum of 10% return on your investment after the 5 years is up. The rest is taken by the bank.

Generally these types of GICs also include a minimum rate of return, making these types of GICs more interesting to invest in. Do your own research if you want to invest in GICs. There are a lot of options, and depending on your needs you may come to a different conclusion than a bank employee would.

Personally I am not a fan of GICs. Anything that locks in your money is not a high ranking choice for me. Even "cashable" GICs often lack a decent rate of return to make them an attractive option for me. Much like savings bonds, if you do not like risk, want to ensure some type of a return on your investment and have no short-to-medium term need for your money then a GIC may be a great investment vehicle for you.

7.4 Stocks

When people think of stocks, they think of the classic "buy low, sell high" adage. This has worked well for a lot of people, but it's also a strategy that needs a lot of nurturing to bear any realistic return on investment. If you know what you are doing, you can make a killing, but since stocks also tend to be more driven by company news, a lot more attention needs to be paid to each stock you own. If you have multiple stocks in multiple companies, the need for monitoring can grow pretty quickly.

7.4.1 Embrace The Dividend

There is a secret about stocks that many people don't know; *you do not need to buy low and sell high in order to make money in the stock market.*

Stocks that offer a *dividend* will pay **you** just for owning them! A *dividend* is a payment made to owners of a stock, usually on a quarterly or monthly basis. Most dividends give on average a 2.8% return, but some can go as high as 5%.

Some people argue that you can make more money by buying and selling these stocks instead of the buy-and-hold strategy that dividend investors often take. My personal opinion is that it is better to stick with the buy-and-hold strategy with dividend stocks rather than the buy-low, sell-high strategy. Why is that? Let me quote one of the arguably most successful investors up to this point in history, Warren Buffett:

> Rule No. 1: Never lose money. Rule No. 2: Never forget rule No. 1.

If you have a stock that is paying you for holding on to it, why would you want to sell? Remember that most stock brokers charge you *per transaction*, so there is some economic incentive to hold on to the stock. Also for Canadians there is a tax break, similar to, but separate from the capital gains tax exemption, that offers incentives for receiving payments from dividends versus buying and selling stocks on the open market.

Another way to look at dividends is that the payments arrive *without you doing a single thing*. This is literally the definition of a passive income!

There are a multitude of books on the subject of stocks and investing but I would recommend one in particular, especially if you are Canadian[6]: *The Idiot Millionaire* by Derek Foster. I am a big fan of Derek's work and I think that his books are a must read for anyone who wants to get into dividend stock investing.

So should you just go and pick any stock that pays dividends? No. Some dividend stocks have a habit of cutting their dividend yields or stopping their dividend programs completely, so you do want to be aware of the stocks that you want to buy into. A little research can go a long way here.

If you do decide to invest in dividend stocks, then you may want to look at a company that offers both a *dividend re-investment plan (DRIP)* and a *stock purchase plan (SPP)*. There are not that many stocks that offer these options compared to the vast number of stocks available in the markets today, but there is a very good reason to find stocks that offer a DRIP and SPP. Why is this important? Why, the

---

[6]US readers will find it equally enlightening as well, but most of Derek's points are geared towards Canadian investors.

ability to re-invest your dividend earnings to buy more shares of course! And at a discount no less! Think of it as compounding the purchases of the stock in order to easily maximize your earning potential.

A SPP allows you to buy more stock directly from the company, bypassing a broker. You often get the stock at a slight discount as well, anywhere from 2% - 5%. Most SPPs also allow for partial stock purchases, meaning that you can own a fractional share of a stock. Even these fractional shares earn you a dividend, helping to grow your return over time!

The real value comes from the fact that you are compounding your investment over time, usually quarterly but some stocks pay monthly as well. Remember, you are going to be re-investing your dividends back into the same stock allowing you to purchase new stock with no further investment on your part. This is a lower risk strategy than trying to buy and sell stocks on the open market and it offers some pretty steady growth opportunities. Dividend payments also carry a much lower tax rate and have some very nice tax exemptions for Canadians, making them a very attractive option to add to your money tree's investment soil.

What about Mutual Funds?

Mutual Funds work with a common pool of money from many different investors that a fund manager then invests into a combination of stocks, bonds and other investment vessels. Think of a mutual fund as a type of buffet for investing where someone else does the hard work for you and a bunch of like-minded individuals.

161

Often times when you are working with a financial planner, they will often try to "sell" a particular set of funds to you. This is how these planners are often paid, by getting people to buy the mutual funds they advertise. The financial planners get paid by the fund companies for bringing in new money for the fund. A mutual fund has a manager who is responsible for the fund. This can be an individual or a company, but the point is that you do not have to manage the lower level details of the investments that make up the fund.

Everything I have covered so far in this chapter could potentially be handled by the manager of a mutual fund. So there is an advantage in that a lot of the legwork is done for you. If you like control, some funds let you decide on specific industries or areas of the stock market you want to buy into for your fund, giving you a sense of more control over the fund. Granted this is not the same as buying the stock yourself, but you do save brokerage fees this way.

The disadvantage that most mutual funds have, in my opinion, is that you often have little control over where your money is going. In addition, some funds have minimum periods that you need to stay in for before you can access your returns. Other funds have a minimum amount you need to invest before you can join the fund.

If you want to have more of a say in where your money is being invested, then a mutual fund may not be to your liking. I had a friend who met with a financial advisor who asked him if he had any moral objections to where his money was going to be invested.

This particular individual was known for providing good returns and had a high minimum principle required for investments made through him. Kudos to this individual for asking the question, but when I was told the story it certainly did not sit well with me that such individuals are so cavalier in their investment options for their clients. To be fair it is very, very hard to find any type of investment vessel that does not have some type of controversy attached to it. Use your own judgment and do your own research if this possibility bothers you.

Mutual funds are a good option if you have no idea where to start outside of Forex. If you do decide to go with a mutual fund, try to learn as much as you can about the fund including how the fund is structured, what are the markets, stocks, options, etc that make up the fund. Since mutual funds are usually comprised of multiple stocks (for example) pick one or two of those stocks that you are not familiar with and try to understand how they perform. Apply some of the indicators I have covered in chapters 4 and 5 to see if the fund is doing better or worse than investments in these companies on their own. That's one advantage that technical indicators have, they can be applied to different types of markets, not just the Forex.

7.5 Understand The Money Tree

As I mentioned at the beginning of this chapter, there really is no "perfect" investment solution. Some people may hit it off with a particular system, be it stocks, Forex, futures, commodities, gold, real estate, etc, but for the rest of us it is a good idea to mix things up. But eating everything you can get your hands on can also give you quite the stomach ache! Here are some things to consider when growing your money tree.

Let Your Money Work For You

If you need to babysit your investments, then it will quickly feel like another full time job! If you feel like you are spending more time managing your money than working at your full time job, you will quickly lose interest and your money tree will grow slower than you may have hoped.

Savings bonds and GICs require no extra effort on your part aside from meeting the minimum requirement to invest, keeping them for a specific time period to maximize returns and (in the case of savings bonds) making sure you purchase them at the right time of year. Dividend stocks do require you to put some more effort in, including finding an appropriate company to invest in.

Managing Forex trades, especially in the beginning, is going to be a huge time sink until you get your Forex groove on. Forex definitely takes more time than the other options I've covered in this chapter, but it also has the potential for greater rewards. Don't try to invest in multiple currency pairs, since each pair has its own unique drivers and characteristics. Focus on one pair and find success there. Over time you may explore others, but initially you should stick with one.

Pace Yourself

The most common investment idiom is "Don't put all your eggs in one basket", which is sound advice when you are talking about investments. Of course the opposite is also true; don't spread yourself out too thin! But isn't that the whole point of diversification, to spread your money out across different investment options?

As we have seen above, different investments require different levels of attention as well as different levels of risk. Trying to invest in everything I have covered in this chapter all at once is going to be very, very overwhelming, very, very quickly. Start with something simple, like a savings bond or "cashable" GIC, just to ensure that you have some money saved away that you can access without penalty if the need arises. The idea is that you want to have some type of guaranteed investment option to help grow your money tree, especially when first starting out. These types of investments are low maintenance and are useful to keep your interest high in growing your money tree because you will start to see real returns with no effort.

Next I would focus on finding a few good dividend stocks that offer DRIPs and SPPs in order to continue the growth of passive income. DRIP stocks will take some legwork to find, but they are very much worth it in my opinion since you can start to see results in as little as a month. Also, once you have some initial shares purchased, they require very little maintenance.

You should be using a practice account for trading Forex during all this time as well. Don't go live with Forex until you have a sufficient understanding of how different currency pairs behave, but that doesn't mean you should wait to start growing your money tree!

If you want your money tree to be successful then it boils down to

Investment Option	Risk	Average Return Per Year
Savings Bonds	Low	1.4%
GICs (Non-Cashable)	Low	1.4%
Dividend Stocks	Medium	2% - 3%
Forex	High	20%

Table 7.1: Risk And Return For Popular Investment Options

this - if you try to do everything at once you will likely fail. An even worse possibility is that you will get frustrated, lose your patience and then start making bad decisions with your investments. Next thing you know is that you start losing money, panic and lose even more. Don't burn yourself out, growing a money tree is more like running a marathon rather than the 100m sprint.

7.6   Risk Matrix

Table 7.1 gives a listing of the different investment options I have covered in this section along with the risk associated with them. Based on your personal needs, appetite for risk and level of control you want to exercise, your money tree will look a lot different than mine or anyone else's. That is the point, a money tree should be what **you** need it to be. Take pride in it and it will bear fruit for you.

The rate of return for Forex trading varies based on the skill of the trader, but most "successful" traders report earnings of 20% per year or more.

7.7 Summary

If the only thing you get out of this chapter is to not put all your money into trading the Forex, then I have done my job. People that are new to trading the Forex think that the only thing they need is to invest in a few different currencies and they have "diversified". Sadly this is not the case. I have listed the other options that I am familiar with, but this is by no means an exhaustive list. Find what appeals to you the most and question everything. Remember, nobody has a more vested interest in your money tree than you do!

People are blinded by the "new and shiny" investment options that they read about and think that this is the only investment worth pursuing. Sadly a lot of authors on the market today make it seem that the topics they cover really **are** only thing worth doing! While it can be true that people can find great success by sticking to one of these investment options, more often than not it is not going to be sustainable for the long term. Diversification is key to maintaining a stable financial future and for having a healthy money tree.

As with everything in this book, use your own best judgment and take it slow. There are a lot of different options when it comes to growing your money tree. Don't put everything into a single investment option and don't try to use every investment option available to you all at once. Remember, too much of a good thing *can* hurt you.

In the next part of the book I will start exploring one of the most interesting[7] forms of AI available today - *Genetic Algorithms.*

---

[7]In my own humble opinion, of course.

Part II

Enrich The Soil With Intelligence

CHAPTER 8

Growing Intelligence

In this chapter I am going to explore how one particular branch of artificial intelligence, *genetic algorithms*, works. This is not going to be a thorough discussion on this topic by a long shot; this is intended to be a high level overview to help you get an understanding of what genetic algorithms are, how they work and why they are useful for solving a particular type of problem. Once you have a basic understanding of how they work, it will be easier to show you how I have used them in helping me find trading strategies for the Forex.

Once you have a basic understanding of how GAs work, it will be easier for me to show you how I have used them in helping me find winning trade strategies for Forex trading. With that in mind, let's dive right in!

8.1 Overview of Genetic Algorithms

Genetic Algorithms (GAs) are part of a branch of artificial intelligence research known as *Evolutionary Algorithms*. Essentially GAs are a type of search algorithm[1] that tries to mimic the laws of natural selection when performing the search.

The way GAs solve a problem is pretty natural and easy to follow, no math or computer science degree required.

8.1.1 Finding A Problem To Solve

First off, GAs do not solve just any type of problem. Unlike something like a neural network that tries to mimic the human brain, or an expert system that tries to mimic the decisions a human would make. See, not all artificial intelligence is about bringing about the end of humankind with super-intelligent machines!

GAs excel with problems that are able to test whether or not a given solution solves said problem. In addition to that, GAs need to be able to measure how well solutions compare to one another. This is because GAs want to find the "best" solution for a given problem from a collection of proposed solutions.

8.1.2 How GAs Work

When working with a GA, you don't just start anywhere. Well, actually, yes you do! GAs often start with a set of random solutions to the problem that they are trying to solve, test them, sort them and

---

[1]An algorithm is a step-by-step plan for solving a problem, often by using a computer.

then apply some evolution à la Charles Darwin. Each evolution to the solution set is where the solutions from the previous generation try to mate, mutate and survive in order to make it to the next generation. This process repeats until a solution is found or a certain number of generations are created.

A more formal overview of how GAs work is as follows:

1. Start with a fixed number of random solutions.

2. Evaluate each solution in the set, measuring how well it solves the problem. Call this score its "fitness".

3. Sort the solutions by fitness from best to worst.

   a) Select a certain percentage of the best solutions, say the best 5%, and copy these to the next generation of solutions completely unchanged.

   b) Go over the remaining solutions one at a time.

      i. Randomly decide whether or not to *mate*[2] it with another solution.

         • If no mating is decided, prepare to copy the solution to the next generation.

         • If mating is decided, select a favorable solution from the current set of solutions and mate the two solutions using a known process, producing offspring that can be copied to the next generation.

      ii. For each solution[3], decide whether or not the solution should be mutated.

---

[2]See Section 8.4.1

[3]Each child must be evaluated individually if two solutions mated in the previous step

- If no mutation is decided, copy the solution to the next generation unchanged.

- If mutation is selected, mutate the solution using a known process and copy the mutated solution to the next generation.

c) Repeat this process until the new set of solutions has the same size as the current set of solutions.

d) Replace the existing set of solutions with the new generation of solutions, discarding the old set.

4. Repeat this evolution process until a solution has been found, or a maximum number of evolutions are performed.

Not too shabby. Don't worry if the discretion above seems a little tricky to follow, I will be going over each of these steps in a lot more detail later on.

8.1.3 Who uses GAs?

So how are GAs used today? One use for GAs is for finding solutions for scheduling problems. A classic example is trying to make sure all the students in a school can enroll for all their courses without any conflicts. GAs have also been used for things like antenna design, circuit board layout, crafting optical lenses, race car design, and a lot more. I personally have used them for solving routing problems (the classic *Traveling Salesman Problem* for the computer scientist types out there) and I currently use them for finding trading strategies for Forex, so they are pretty flexible.

GAs are not terribly complex on the surface (especially compared with other artificial intelligence techniques such as neural networks), but as they say, the devil is in the details. The next few sections will go through the various components that make up a GA, starting with *fitness*.

8.2 Finding Fitness

When we talk about a solution to a problem in the context of GAs, we often refer to its *fitness*. How well does a particular solution solve the problem? This implies that a solution already exists, so why not just use that one? It turns out that these "ideal" solutions may not be ideal at all! As we learned in school, there are many different ways to solve a problem, and GAs can help you find a better solution, or confirm that the solution you have is an "ideal" one.

Let's use an example of designing a new antenna; we already know how to design an antenna but we're curious if there is a design that gives us better signal strength using fewer materials. We already have an existing design which works and seems optimal, but more importantly we have a way of measuring how well a particular antenna design functions.

For Forex, I have used two different ways to measure fitness. The first was simply measuring the net profit - how much did my strategy earn me over a certain number of periods? This one was simple as it was just checking each solution's net profit and using that as the fitness. The larger the net profit, the more "fit" the solution was deemed to be.

The second approach I took was trying to meet a profit target - say a 25% profit over a specific period. Of course the old mantra of any investor rings true here: "past performance is not an indicator of

175

future results", but sometimes these past trends *do* continue for short periods into the future. That is when things get interesting, and by interesting, I mean that is when you can make some profit!

Calculating the fitness of a solution is a task performed by a *fitness function*, which is just a sub-routine that is responsible for evaluating a solution. One thing you should keep in mind when writing a fitness function is that you want it to be as efficient as possible, because it is the most called upon function in the entire program! Remember, each offspring and each mutation must be evaluated using the fitness function, and this is repeated for each new generation.

Measuring how well a solution solves a problem can be tricky at times, but it is not the hardest part of writing a GA. Artificial intelligence in general is part art form, part science, and GAs are no exception. In order to use a GA, you must be able to represent a solution in a form that is easy to manipulate with mating and mutation functions. This process is called *encoding*, and it is where the "art form" comes into play.

8.3 Encoding Solutions

Encoding is the heart and soul of not just GAs, but of any artificial intelligence system. Encoding is a fancy way of saying that you have something you want to make "computer friendly". In the case of a GA, you want to be able to encode a solution, and then use this encoded solution for fitness evaluation, mating and mutation.

Books dedicated to GAs will cover encoding over multiple chapters, since there are different encoding strategies that can be used to encode pretty much anything you can imagine. For this book, however, I will keep things simple and tell you about *binary encoding*.

8.3.1 Binary Encoding

Binary encoding is probably the simplest encoding strategy available. Yes *that* binary - the ones and zeros that you often see portrayed in cheesy computer hacking movies.

Binary encoding is incredibly useful since you can, quite literally, encode any problem in a binary string! All you need to know is how to interpret those ones and zeros. It usually helps to visualize what the binary string looks like, since that way you know how you can manipulate it with mating and mutation. Figure 8.1 gives an example of what a 10 digit binary encoded string might look like.

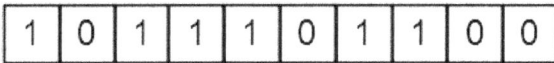

1	0	1	1	1	0	1	1	0	0

Figure 8.1: A sample ten digit binary encoded string

There are no maximum or minimum lengths when it comes to a binary encoded string; it really depends on what you need to encode. For example, if my solution defines the use of two different moving averages (hint, hint), then I might have a binary encoded string where a certain number of digits is the binary representation of the number of periods to use for one moving average. The other digits may include the binary representation of the number of periods to use for the other moving average. I might even go so far as to interpret two more digits to represent whether or not each moving average is either a SMA or an EMA.

Once an encoding strategy has been determined, you can start to focus on mating and mutating the solutions. In the case of mating, you also need a way to choose which other solution you want to mate with. Sure you could do it randomly, but the results would not be great. Remember, we want to select "good" solutions to mate with in order to find an even better solution.

8.4 Selection

Darwin's famous theory of evolution says that the fittest will survive. With a GA, you start with a bunch of random solutions to a problem, evaluate them using a fitness function and then rank them according to their fitness from best to worst. We then "evolve" this solution set, which involves mating and mutating some of these solutions while leaving others unchanged.

So evolution in terms of a GA means what exactly? As we saw in Section 8.1.2, during the evolution process a solutions will be processed according to one of three rules:

1. Move over the "elite" solution to the new generation unchanged.

2. Mate a solution with another solution to produce offspring, randomly mutating these offspring before copying them to the next generation.

3. Randomly mutate the solution before copying it to the new generation.

Mutation will be covered in it's own section, so instead I'll cover the first two options, starting with copying over the "elite" solutions.

178

8.4.1 Elitism and Mating

The first option is known as *elitism*, and it really is as harsh as some high school cliques can be. "Elite" solutions are taken from the top n-percent of the solutions and copied to the next generation completely unchanged. The theory is that if they are the best, then they should be able to hold their own in the next generation.

The second option is (surprise, surprise) more complex. The reason it is more complex is that you don't want to just randomly select two solutions to mate, since that flies in the face of Darwin's theory of survival of the fittest! What we want is a pseudo-random selection, one that favors better solutions when selecting a mate. To solve this dilemma, computer scientists have come up with a few different ways to perform this pseudo-random selection. *Tournament selection* is one such algorithm, and it is both efficient and fast.

8.4.2 Tournament Selection

The way *tournament selection* works is that you randomly select a solution from the collection. Next, you pick another random solution and compare it to the first one. The solution with the best fitness wins and moves on to the next round. This process repeats for another two-to-four rounds and with each round the solution with the better fitness moves on to the next round. The winning solution at the end of this mini tournament is the one you use to mate with.

Other pseudo-selection algorithms include *roulette-wheel selection*, *stochastic sampling*, *truncation selection*, and many more. The point to remember is that we want to improve our solutions, so mating with "good" solutions is preferred to random hook-ups.

179

Of course once we have selected two solutions the big question remains; how do we plan on mating these two solutions?

8.5 Mating

Remember when I said that binary encoding would make it easier to mate and mutate solutions? Well I'm about to prove it. How so you ask? As I discussed in Section 8.4, there are three ways to get a solution into the next generation of solutions. One of the items in the list was about mating two solutions from the current generation.

Let's assume that we've ran our tournament selection and we now have two solutions we want to mate. Let's call them s_1 and s_2. Since we are using a binary encoding for these solutions, we know that each solution has a fixed length. Let's call that length l. Now in order to "mate" these two solutions, we pick a random number between 1 and l, and call this random number n. Then to create our offspring we start by taking portions of each solution and merging them together.

The first offspring is constructed with the first n digits from s_1, and the remaining $(l-n)$ digits come from s_2 starting at the $(n+1)$th digit. The second child works the same way, but we use the first n digits from s_2 and the last $(l-n)$ digits from s_1. Confusing? Absolutely. So let's look a how this is done using pictures.

Figure 8.2 shows two binary encoded strings representing two solutions, s_1 and s_2, that we want to mate:

Each solution is 10 digits long (i.e. $l = 10$), so we start by picking a random number between 1 and 10. 6 sounds like a good choice, so we use that for the value n. Following the steps outlined above, the first step is to take the first 6 digits from s_1 and the last $10 - 6 = 4$

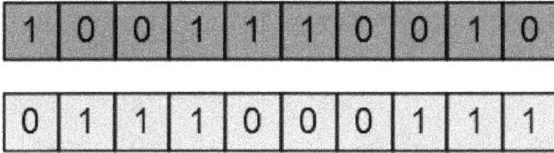

Figure 8.2: Two 10-digit binary encoded strings selected for mating

digits from s_2 and combine them. Figure 8.3 shows how this is done.

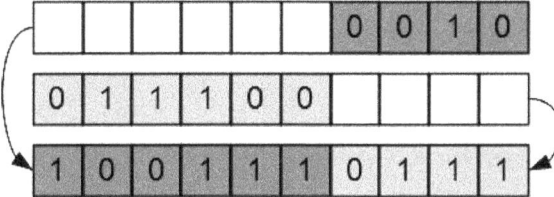

Figure 8.3: Creating the first offspring from the two solutions

Great! Now we have created our first child solution! Now let us repeat the process and build our second child.

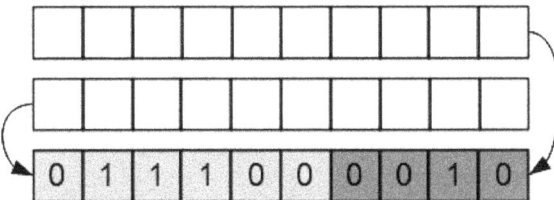

Figure 8.4: Creating the second child from the two solutions

As we can see from Figure 8.4, we take the remaining values and combine them, starting with the second parent solution and giving us our second and final child solution.

Normally you decide to mate two solutions together about 60 - 80% of the time. The remaining 20 - 40% of the time you just randomly select a gene and copy it over. Well, almost. There is still a small chance that something will change for any of the solutions copied over to the new generation. Any "non-elite" solution is subject to *mutation* before being copied to the next generation, including the offspring of two mated solutions.

8.6 Mutation

If you have seen the X-Men movies or read nearly any type of comic book, you know what mutation is. Something changes and the individual gets some type of super power. Unfortunately that is not how mutation works in GAs. Mutating a solution does not suddenly make it a "super solution" that can power through any problem, although that would be pretty cool if it could.

Mutation in GAs is much simpler and far less exciting. It usually boils down to just flipping the bit on one of the values in a binary encoded solution string. When I say "flip the bit" I mean change a zero to a one or a one to a zero. The bit to flip is randomly selected. In this case this is a true random selection, since there is no "best bit" in an encoded solution. Figure 8.5 shows a simple mutation of the 8th digit in an encoded solution.

Mutation is a random process and can be applied to any non-elite solution that is being brought into the next generation's collection of solutions. Does that mean that every solution in the new generation is

| 1 | 0 | 1 | 1 | 1 | 0 | 1 | 1 | 0 | 0 |

| 1 | 0 | 1 | 1 | 1 | 0 | 1 | 0 | 0 | 0 |

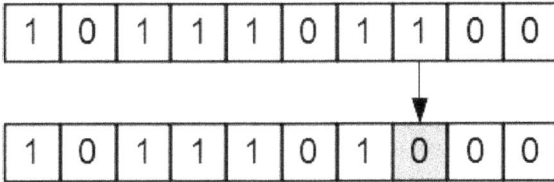

Figure 8.5: Mutating a random digit in a binary encoded solution string

a mutant? No. You generally only mutate about 5% of the non-elite solutions being copied to the next generation, including any offspring after mating two solutions.

I'd like to close out this chapter by standardizing my terminology a bit. I have tried to stay as straightforward as possible for this rather technical topic, but if you decide to go read up on GAs from a more technical book, you may quickly get lost in the terminology that they use. Let me clear that up now.

8.7 Populations, Chromosomes and Genes! Oh my!

In a more traditional book on genetic algorithms, you will see terms like *population*, *chromosome*, *gene* and others. Let me try my best to quickly define each of these in terms of the descriptions I have given so far in this chapter.

Population A *population* is a collection of solutions. The population is evolved through elitism, copying, mating and mutation as described earlier, but the definition of the population is a collection of these solutions.

Chromosome A *chromosome* is a container for an encoded solution. In computer science there is the concept of *object oriented programming* where there are objects that you can perform actions on, like a car which has a horn that you can push to make a sound. A chromosome is a wrapper around a solution, but it provides actions that allow you to mate with other chromosomes, mutate this chromosome or retrieve its fitness.

Gene A *gene* is another name for an encoded solution, such as the binary encoded string that I covered earlier. It is normally a trait of a chromosome and not a stand-alone entity.

Crossover *Crossover* is another term commonly used to refer to the process of mating of two chromosomes. *Crossover Rate* refers to the probability of a chromosome being selected to be mated during an evolution.

8.8 Summary

I know that this chapter had a lot of information you may not be familiar with, especially if you do not have a background in computer science. Hang in there, it does get easier. In the next chapter I will take you through a very basic GA implementation that shows how you can grow the phrase *"Hello, world!"* starting from a set random characters. It's an interesting problem on its own, but it will also help to give a concrete example to the concepts covered in this chapter.

Chapter 9

"Hello, World!", Genetic Algorithm Style

In this chapter, we'll take a more practical approach to genetic algorithms (GAs) by providing a simple program to show how they actually work. If you are not a programmer and have no interest in reading programming code, then please feel free to skip this chapter.

For those of you who are interested, I will be using Python[1] as my language of choice, due to its universal appeal and ease of reading[2]. I am assuming that you have some rudimentary programming knowledge or know how to read code, so I will just be focusing on the logic how the GA works and not how to program in Python.

---

[1]Python 3.0
[2]If you want to see other languages, check out: *https://github.com/jsvazic/GAHelloWorld*

9.1 Say "Hello, world!"

In computer programming, one of the first things you learn how to do is to write a program that says "Hello, world!". So I thought what better way to showcase how a GA works than having it *solve* the problem of converting a bunch of random characters into the phrase "Hello, world!"? First I will provide the complete code listing, then I will dive into the details explaining how the GA was implemented.

9.2 Code

Listing 9.1 provides a Python 3.0 implementation of the "Hello, world!" program:

```
"""
A python 3.0 script that demonstrates a simple "Hello,
    world!"
application using genetic algorithms (GAs).
@author: John Svazic
"""

from random import (choice, random, randint)

class Chromosome:
    _target_gene = "Hello, world!"

    @staticmethod
    def _update_fitness(gene):
        fitness = 0
        for a, b in zip(gene, Chromosome._target_gene):
            fitness += abs(ord(a) - ord(b))

        return fitness
```

```python
    def __init__(self, gene):
        self.gene = gene
        self.fitness = Chromosome._update_fitness(gene)

    def mate(self, mate):
        pivot = randint(0, len(self.gene) - 1)
        gene1 = self.gene[:pivot] + mate.gene[pivot:]
        gene2 = mate.gene[:pivot] + self.gene[pivot:]

        return Chromosome(gene1), Chromosome(gene2)

    def mutate(self):
        gene = list(self.gene)
        idx = randint(0, len(gene) - 1)
        gene[idx] = chr(randint(32, 121))

        return Chromosome(''.join(gene))

    @staticmethod
    def generate_random():
        gene = []
        for x in range(len(Chromosome._target_gene)):
            gene.append(chr(randint(32, 121)))

        return Chromosome(''.join(gene))

class Population:
    def __init__(self, size, crossover, elitism,
        mutation):
        self.elitism = elitism
        self.mutation = mutation
        self.crossover = crossover

        buf = []
```

```
        for i in range(size):
            buf.append(Chromosome.generate_random())

        self.population = list(
            sorted(buf, key=lambda x: x.fitness))

    def _tournament_selection(self):
        best = choice(self.population)

        for i in range(3):
            ctndr = choice(self.population)

            if (ctndr.fitness < best.fitness):
                best = ctndr

        return best

    def evolve(self):
        size = len(self.population)
        idx = int(round(size * self.elitism))
        buf = self.population[:idx]

        while (idx < size):
            if random() <= self.crossover:
                parent1 = self.population[idx]
                parent2 = self.tournament_selection()
                children = parent1.mate(parent2)
                for c in children:
                    if random() <= self.mutation:
                        buf.append(c.mutate())
                    else:
                        buf.append(c)
                idx += 2
            else:
                if random() <= self.mutation:
```

```
            buf.append(
                self.population[idx].mutate())
        else:
            buf.append(self.population[idx])
        idx += 1

    self.population = list(sorted(buf[:size],
        key=lambda x: x.fitness))

if __name__ == "__main__":
    pop = Population(2048, 0.75, 0.1, 0.15)

    for i in range(1, 16385):
        print("Generation %d: %s" % (i,
            pop.population[0].gene))

        if pop.population[0].fitness == 0:
            break
        else:
            pop.evolve()
    else:
        print("Maximum generations reached.")
```

Listing 9.1: Python Implementation Of "Hello, world!" Using Genetic Algorithms

Now that we have the complete program, allow me to walk you through its implementation of the GA.

9.3 Rules

Right off the bat, there are a few rules that were defined for this program:

- Each solution must have exactly 13 characters

189

- Each solution can only contain US English letters, numbers and punctuation

- The final solution must be found within $16,384$ evolutions or the program will exit

As you can see I have broken the code up into two classes:

- Chromosome

- Population

This way I can separate out the code into logical groups, and have methods that act on their internal state. Let's move on and examine the Chromosome class.

9.4 Chromosome

The Chromosome class is nothing more than a container for a solution (called the *gene* for the remainder of this chapter) and some methods that calculate the fitness, mate the Chromosome with another Chromosome, and mutate the Chromosome.

Every gene is stored within a Chromosome, and every Chromosome is immutable. This is a fancy way of saying that if I call mutate or mate on a Chromosome instance, a new Chromosome will be created and that is what these methods will return. Since Chromosome instances are immutable, it makes sense to pre-compute the fitness since it will never change for the lifetime of the Chromosome.

One important thing to note is that we are not using binary encoded strings for the gene. It turns out it was easier just to work with the gene directly as it is, since it is a string and in Python we can treat those strings as an array of characters.

190

9.4.1 Fitness

So as we discussed in the last chapter, finding out how to measure the fitness of a Chromosome is one of the key tasks when using a GA. In Listing 9.2 we can see the code used to calculate the fitness of a solution:

```
_target_gene = "Hello, world!"

@staticmethod
def _update_fitness(gene):
    fitness = 0
    for a, b in zip(gene, Chromosome._target_gene):
        fitness += abs(ord(a) - ord(b))

    return fitness
```

Listing 9.2: Fitness Function For "Hello, world!"

The _target_gene is a constant representing the ideal solution to the problem. The _update_fitness(gene) method takes a solution (stored in the gene variable in the Chromosome instance) and compares it with the target string. The way it does this is by subtracting the decimal ASCII value for each character from the decimal ASCII value for the target string and take the absolute value of that difference. The sum of these deltas are then summed up to achieve the final fitness value of the solution. So the smaller the fitness, the better the solution. The idea is that the "perfect" solution should have a fitness of zero. Keep in mind that the only requirement for a fitness function is being able to determine how good a solution is, not what values constitute a "good" fitness. As long as we can sort the fitness from best to worst, the actual range of values does not matter.

9.4.2 Mating

Even though we are not using a binary encoded string to model our solutions, each solution is still represented as an array so the method that we discussed in Section 8.5 can still be applied to these solutions. Listing 9.3 shows the code for the mate method:

```
def mate(self, mate):
    pivot = randint(0, len(self.gene) - 1)
    gene1 = self.gene[:pivot] + mate.gene[pivot:]
    gene2 = mate.gene[:pivot] + self.gene[pivot:]

    return Chromosome(gene1), Chromosome(gene2)
```

Listing 9.3: mate Method For "Hello, world!"

As you can see, the mate method is fairly straightforward. Given a Chromosome instance, we call the mate method passing in another Chromosome instance. A random index is selected from 1 to the length of the gene and then stored in a variable called pivot. Then two new genes are created using the technique described in Section 8.5, resulting in two new Chromosome instances.

9.4.3 Mutation

Similar to the mate method, the mutate method generates a new Chromosome instance when it is called. Listing 9.4 shows the relevant code:

```
def mutate(self):
    gene = list(self.gene)
    idx = randint(0, len(gene) - 1)
    gene[idx] = chr(randint(32, 121))
```

192

```
return Chromosome('' .join(gene))
```

Listing 9.4: mutate Method For "Hello, world!"

Back in Section 8.6 I described mutation as flipping a random bit in the gene from a zero to a one and vice versa. This works if you are dealing with a binary encoded string, but in the case of our "Hello, world!" program we are using a string instead. So what can we do? Well, we already know that the gene only contains letters, numbers and punctuation, so we adjust our mutation algorithm slightly:

1. Convert the gene to an array of characters

2. Select a random index to "mutate"

3. Pick a new character at random from the collection of valid characters

4. Overwrite the value at the index with the new character

5. Create a new Chromosome instance with the new gene

And with that we have described the basic building blocks for evaluating and generating new solutions using the Chromosome class. Up next is the Population class, which acts as the container for our Chromosome instances as well as the main controller of the evolution of these Chromosome instances.

9.5 Population

The Population class is really nothing more than a class that maintains a collection of Chromosomes, with a few methods thrown in to help with sorting and evolution.

193

9.5.1 Initial Population

Back in Section 8.1.2 I spoke about how every GA program starts with an initial population of random solutions. That's exactly what the __init__ method is for. This method is called when you create a new instance of the Population class. Listing 9.5 shows the relevant code:

```
def __init__(self, size, crossover, elitism,
    mutation):
    self.elitism = elitism
    self.mutation = mutation
    self.crossover = crossover

    buf = []
    for i in range(size):
        buf.append(Chromosome.generate_random())

    self.population = list(
        sorted(buf, key=lambda x: x.fitness))
```

Listing 9.5: ___init___ Method For The Population Class

In order to instantiate a Population object, you need to specify a few parameters. The size of the population as well as the crossover, elitism and mutation rates. These last 3 rates are measured as percentages and are used by the Population.evolve() method when evolving the set of Chromosomes for the next generation.

The __init__() method generates a fixed number of random Chromosome instances and then sorts them based on their fitness, going from the smallest to largest.

9.5.2 Evolution

Evolving a new generation is really a multi-step process: determine
how many "elite" Chromosomes to keep, determine whether to mate a
Chromosome or not, and whether or not to mutate these Chromosomes
before moving them to the next generation. Listing 9.6 shows the
relevant code for the evolve() method:

```python
def evolve(self):
    size = len(self.population)
    idx = int(round(size * self.elitism))
    buf = self.population[:idx]

    while (idx < size):
        if random() <= self.crossover:
            parent1 = self.population[idx]
            parent2 = self.tournament_selection()
            children = parent1.mate(parent2)
            for c in children:
                if random() <= self.mutation:
                    buf.append(c.mutate())
                else:
                    buf.append(c)
            idx += 2
        else:
            if random() <= self.mutation:
                buf.append(
                    self.population[idx].mutate())
            else:
                buf.append(self.population[idx])
            idx += 1
```

```
self.population = list(sorted(buf[:size],
    key=lambda x: x.fitness))
```

Listing 9.6: evolve() Method For The Population Class

Unlike the Chromosome class, the Population class is not immutable. That means that each time the evolve method is called, the collection of solutions stored within the Population instance changes, so no new Population instance is created. This is a subtle difference and has no impact on how the program works, but I thought it would be good to note the difference.

The process of evolution is pretty straightforward. Start off by creating a new collection for the next generation of Chromosomes and copy over the top subset of Chromosomes based on the elitisim ratio.

Next, the method iterates over the remaining Chromosomes and randomly decides whether or not to mate each one based on the crossover ratio. If mating is deemed necessary, another Chromosome is selected[3] to mate with. Next, the Chromosome.mate() method is called to generate the offspring. After mating, the method randomly decides whether or not to mutate the offspring. This is done for each child independently, so it is possible that both offspring will be mutated.

If no mating is determined, then the current Chromosome is randomly mutated before moving on to the next generation. In both

---

[3]The selection algorithm will be covered in Section 9.5.3.

the individual and offspring mutations, the Chromosome.mutate() method is used to perform the mutation[4].

This entire process repeats until the new generation has at least the same number of Chromosomes as the original population. Once that limit has been reached, the new generation is trimmed if necessary and then sorted by fitness. The current generation is replaced with this new generation and the method returns.

9.5.3 Selection

In Section 8.4 I mentioned a few different ways to select a random solution from a collection of solutions, but I explained *tournament selection* specifically. Listing 9.7 outlines a tournament selection implementation used in the "Hello, world!" example:

```
def _tournament_selection(self):
    best = choice(self.population)

    for i in range(3):
        ctndr = choice(self.population)

        if (ctndr.fitness < best.fitness):
            best = ctndr

    return best
```

Listing 9.7: Tournament Selection Method For The Population Class

The approach used is relatively straightforward. A Chromosome is randomly selected from the population, and it is labeled as the *best* one found so far. Another random Chromosome is then selected and

---

[4]See Section 9.4.3 for the details of this method.

labeled as the *contender*. The fitness value for the two Chromosomes are compared, and the Chromosome with the better fitness is declared the "best". This process repeats a total of 3 times, finally returning the best Chromosome found.

> **Picking A Tournament Size**
>
> For this particular example I have used a tournament size of 3, but it is not uncommon to see tournament sizes of 5 or 7 used. There are no hard and fast rules in regards to tournament size, just some conventions used by GA researchers.

That really is all there is to the main GA code. There is only one piece of code left to review, namely the main entry point of the program.

9.6   Pulling It All Together

So we have our basic GA building blocks with the Chromsome and Population classes, but how are they used to create a final program? Listing 9.8 gives the relevant code:

```python
if __name__ == "__main__":
    pop = Population(2048, 0.75, 0.1, 0.15)

    for i in range(1, 16385):
        print("Generation %d: %s" % (i,
            pop.population[0].gene))
```

```
    if pop.population[0].fitness == 0:
        break
    else:
        pop.evolve()
else:
    print("Maximum generations reached.")
```

Listing 9.8: Main Application Code for "Hello, World"

The first thing we do is construct a new instance of the `Population` class, pass it the population size as well as the crossover, elitism and mutation rates respectively. This generates the initial population of Chromosomes as described in Section 9.5.1.

I have specified a population size of 2048 Chromosomes, a crossover rate of 75%, an elitism rate of 10% and a mutation rate of 15%. These are common starting values for these parameters, but can be updated depending on how the GA behaves.

After the `Population` is initialized, the evolving begins! The best solution for the current generation is printed along with the generation number. The code then checks the fitness for this "best" solution. If the best solution is found, the loop is stopped and we exit the program. Otherwise, we evolve the population and repeat the print and evaluate steps. This will repeat to a maximum of 16385 evolutions. If no solution is found by then, the program exits with a message indicating this fact.

9.7 Output - What Does It Look Like

So what does the output of this program look like? If you ran this using a Python interpreter, you may get output similar to the following:

199

```
Generation 1: D6][y;Myyhde0
Generation 2: ,[][y;Myyhde0
Generation 3: fpnpl5(yom.j&
Generation 4: _odpP6 iumga!
Generation 5: Ilfhi)#rQera!
Generation 6: Eajxp?!mjnge%
Generation 7: Eajbo,/wered
Generation 8: Hnqip?!snsnd$
Generation 9: Gbibj0!snvqe
Generation 10: Edkiw-!swvme&
Generation 11: Hlknh, snske%
Generation 12: Edkip,(ynska!
Generation 13: Gbkio,!yomqe
Generation 14: Eajlp,!wnskg!
Generation 15: Gcjlp,!wnskg!
Generation 16: Hdkio,!yoskd!
Generation 17: Hdkno,!unrmd!
Generation 18: Hdkno,!unrmd!
Generation 19: Gdklp, wnskd!
Generation 20: Gellp, wnskd!
Generation 21: Gellp, wnskd!
Generation 22: Heklp,!workd!
Generation 23: Heklp,!workd!
Generation 24: Heklo, wnrkd!
Generation 25: Heklo, wnrkd!
Generation 26: Hello,!wormd!
Generation 27: Hello, workd!
Generation 28: Hello, workd!
```

```
Generation 29: Hello, workd!
Generation 30: Hello, workd!
Generation 31: Hello, workd!
Generation 32: Hello, workd!
Generation 33: Hello, workd!
Generation 34: Hello, workd!
Generation 35: Hello, workd!
Generation 36: Hello, workd!
Generation 37: Hello, workd!
Generation 38: Hello, workd!
Generation 39: Hello, workd!
Generation 40: Hello, workd!
Generation 41: Hello, workd!
Generation 42: Hello, workd!
Generation 43: Hello, world!
```

The "best" solution for each generation gets progressively better until the target string, *Hello, world!*, is reached. Sometimes the program can find a solution in as little as 20 generations, while other times it can take a few hundred generations. This is the nature of genetic algorithms, which is partly why I find them so fascinating!

Starting around generation 27, we see the program sticking with one particular solution. One of the reasons for the program getting "stuck" on a solution like is is partly due to the elitism trait that is built into the program. Since *Hello, workd!* is just one character off from the ideal solution, it takes a few more generations for either a random mutation or mating before the program finds the ideal solution and exits. This can take a few generations or a few hundred, depending on the simulation. This is also why I have an upper-limit to the number of evolutions the program will run.

9.8 Summary

As you can see, GAs can solve some pretty unique solutions. Who knew that there was a way to "grow" a phrase? As you can see, GAs are pretty versatile and (hopefully) not too difficult to implement. In the next chapter, I will shift focus away from the implementation details and focus on some strategies you can use to apply GAs to help find Forex trading strategies.

CHAPTER 10

Darwin Meets Dollars

Hopefully the last two chapters have helped you get a sense of how GAs work and where they can help find solutions to problems.

In this chapter I want to give you some design tips and ideas for using genetic algorithms (GAs) to find Forex strategies. Be aware that by their very nature not all strategies will be successful! Of course that is also why you should always test your newfound strategies thoroughly on a practice account before going live.

10.1 Before You Begin...

Naturally you want to jump right in and start modeling solutions for your incredible, never-to-fail trading strategy. Good for you! It's good to be excited about something new, especially when it could change your life for the better.

However, I do want to share a few things you will want to do that are *not* related to GAs. These points have caused me trouble in the past, so I would like to give you a heads up before you take the plunge.

10.1.1 Simulate The Broker

Simulating a broker was the biggest hang-up for me when I first decided to use GAs to find trade strategies. As you are aware, GAs try to come up with a fitness level for a chromosome. This process is repeated because there are many, many chromosomes in a typical GA application with a large population size and an even larger evolution count!

When it comes to strategies for Forex, the fitness level will be determined by executing trades. Since there is no known "perfect solution" for a strategy, it is safe to assume that the maximum evolution count will be hit each time a full GA simulation[1] is run.

I think it is safe to say that you do not want to make all of these trades directly with your broker. Not only would it be costly, it would be pretty slow as well. While practice accounts are great, there are network delays, order execution delays and more that are associated with every trade. So what are you to do? Well, you need to write your own *broker simulator*.

When I made the decision to use a GA to come up with trade strategies, I thought I understood exactly how my broker worked. In my mind it was simple; place a trade and check each data point to see if either the SL or TP triggers were hit. If they were, close out the order and record the resulting profit or loss. Ah, the ignorance of youth.

---

[1]When you use a GA as a stand alone program, it is called a *GA simulation*.

Turns out there are a lot more variables. A lot of this is common sense, but at the time I didn't think that far ahead. For starters, you need to ensure you process the SL triggers first **before** you process any TP trigger. You need to do the calculations ahead of each order being generated to make sure you have sufficient funds to execute the order. Don't forget to model an order class to keep that separate from the broker class! Have you looked at the spread? What about supporting multiple currencies? What's the calculation to determine the profit on an order placed for USD/CAD? Remember the USD is the base currency here, not the quote, so it's not a simple one-pip-equals-10-USD equation like it is for EUR/USD. And so on, and so on...

To put it mildly, there are a lot of variables. The ability to simulate a broker was the most important thing. So before you begin on your adventure where you use GAs to come up with winning trade strategies, make sure you have a fitness function that will let you test those trades. Even before you decide on what your trade strategy will be or how you will encode it, you need to make sure you have some way to test it.

Here's a list that outlines, at a minimum, the features and concepts you need to consider when creating a broker simulator. A lot of them may seem like common sense and there may be some things you feel may be missing, but it will give you a starting point for your own simulator:

- Support multiple currency pairs
- Open and close orders
- Calculate profit/loss for an order
- Determine the maximum units/lots available for an order

- Specify SL and TP triggers
- Process currency pair pricing data, such as OHLC or Candlestick data
- Close orders automatically when a SL or TP trigger is hit

As I mentioned in Section 2.2, most brokers offer a practice account. Use it to better understand how your broker works. You need to have a system to mimic your broker and execute your orders in the same manner as your real broker would. I would literally spend hours upon hours testing with my practice account to better understand my broker and then test my own "broker simulator" making sure it behaved the same way. Without this crucial piece, no amount of awesome GA code will help you find a successful trading strategy.

10.1.2 Check Your Data

Data, the lifeblood of a simulation. Get it right and things go well. Get it wrong or misinterpret it and things can go *subtly* wrong.

In order to test a strategy, you want to use historic data. This process is called "backtesting", and it is incredibly important to do before you make any actual trades. The reason is, of course, you want to confirm any strategies you come up with are profitable. To do this, you need some historic data to test your trades against. Also you will run a lot of trade simulations for each chromosome and for each evolution, so you want some consistent data you can use over and over again.

Sometimes you can get tick-by-tick data, the so-called "real time" data that brokers use. Other times you can only get the OHLC[2] data

---

[2]Open, High, Low, Close

for a specific time period. Regardless of how you get the sample data, always check that it is consistent! I have had data where there have been "holes" in the data, including up to *two consecutive months* missing!

Make sure you know what time zone the historic data is in. Some sources use UTC/Greenwich Mean Time, while others will use your local time zone. Using the wrong time zone can potentially cause issues if you try to filter out weekend data as some sources will include this as well. If they do, then you definitely want to filter it out or you risk skewing any moving average or RSI calculations you may be doing.

Finally, you will want to get the data from a reputable broker or service that provides signal data. This may seem obvious, but there are an awful lot of sources on the Internet that claim to have historic data, only to have absolute garbage. I once purchased a few DVDs worth of historic data that was utterly useless. I'll cover more on that in Chapter 11, so no spoilers here.

Now with all that preamble out of the way, let me walk you through some other considerations when designing your own GA to find successful trade strategies. For the rest of this chapter I will assume you have good sample data and you have a functioning "broker simulator" you can use to successfully backtest your strategies.

10.2 Encoding

In order to find an optimal trading strategy, you need to start with one that you want to improve upon. This is really the heart of the matter, and probably one of the most difficult questions you will have to answer - namely what is a good starting strategy? Not only that, you also need to figure out how to encode it! Thankfully, I have been down this road myself and I want to share my own experiences. Why would I do this? For one very simple reason - I believe in sharing information and helping others. All of this is based on my personal experience, so your experience may vary.

My initial strategy involves trading the crossover of two moving averages and an RSI to maximize profit. I vary two things with each moving average; their type and the number of periods to use for each MA. For the MA type, I choose between the SMA and EMA. The number of periods for each MA ranges from 1 to 32 periods. For the RSI, I also make the number of periods a variable between 1 and 32.

I use a binary encoding to store all these values. Figure 10.1 shows what this encoding looks like:

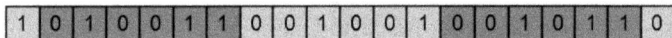

| 1 | 0 | 1 | 0 | 0 | 1 | 1 | 0 | 0 | 1 | 0 | 0 | 1 | 0 | 0 | 1 | 0 | 1 | 1 | 0 |

Figure 10.1: A sample Forex trading strategy gene

The first digit is the type of the first MA[3]. The next six digits are the binary representation of the size of the periods for the first MA. The following six digits are the binary representation of the size of the periods for the RSI. The next six digits are the binary representation of the number of periods for the second MA. Finally, the last digit is the type of the second MA.

This strategy should look familiar to you. Yes, you guessed it! It's the same strategy I used in Chapter 6! I'm constantly testing and re-testing new strategies, but this is the strategy I have come back to

---

[3] $0 = EMA$ and $1 = SMA$

time and time again. It's simple, encodes well, and produces pretty good results most of the time.

The encoding strategy discussed here can easily be adapted to a variety of other technical indicators, so as you grow in your experience with Forex I encourage you to test out new trading strategies. There are a lot of other indicators out there, you may find yourself testing those out instead. Adapt this encoding and test them out! With sample data, the sky's the limit as far as new strategies are concerned.

10.3 Fitness Function

Encoding is good, but figuring out how profitable a strategy is is better. Consider two things when creating a fitness function for testing Forex strategies; what other rules do you have in place in addition to the encoded values and how are you going to measure the fitness of a strategy.

10.3.1 Interpret And Evaluate

In Section 10.2, I use the same indicators I showed you in Chapter 6, but in Chapter 6, I also had other rules in place to help me interpret the signals from the indicators. Rules such as requiring a minimum delta for the moving average crossover and ensuring that the RSI was between certain limits to support a Buy or Sell signal.

> Remember the golden rule in technical Forex trading - never make a trade based on a single indicator! Always have consensus with other indicators before making a trade.

The point is, there is more to the fitness function than just interpreting the encoded values. Remember, there are additional interpretations and rules that need to be interpreted for each potential trade.

10.3.2 Measure The Fitness

Measuring the fitness of a strategy should be simple, right? Just base it on the profit made from some test data. I mean, you *do* want it to make money, right? Actually, this is just one strategy you can use. Another strategy I have used is looking for a certain percentage of return when testing with the training data[4].

So why would this be another option? Let me repeat the mantra of successful investors everywhere:

Past performance is not an indicator of future results.

Just because a strategy was profitable for some training data does not mean it will be successful for future "live" data. For example, if your training data set is too small, you risk overfitting your data and it will not be usable for future trades. If you use a data set that is too large, you may not be able to find a consistent and reliable strategy. A conundrum!

---

[4]I will refer to the data used by the fitness function during the evolutions as the *training data*, just so we're on the same proverbial page.

Beware Of Overfitting!

Over-fitting is a term often used in artificial intelligence to refer to the phenomenon when you manage to find a perfect solution to a problem using the training data, but the solution fails miserably when applied to non-training data. What happens is your system finds a perfect solution to the given set of data, but that solution is very fragile and cannot be applied to anything even slightly different. Sometimes this over fitting is useful, such as when you have the complete set of data your system will ever see! Unfortunately in Forex (or any other financial market) we do not have that luxury.

This is where I decided it was a good idea to target a particular rate of return, rather than try to maximize my profit. I decided to aim for a return rate of 35%. This worked out well for a number of months, but I had to change it due to poor performance. Currently I'm back to using the maximum return.

So what is the best approach? It depends on how the market is reacting and what you feel comfortable with. There really is no right answer here; the reality is you may find something that fits your style of trading better. Unfortunately, there is no silver bullet, so patience and practice are important factors to success.

Let me take everything I have covered so far in this chapter and tie it all together by giving an outline of the main driver for the GA simulation.

10.4 Simulation Driver

There is often a debate amongst GA enthusiasts over what acceptable values for the population size, elitism, crossover and mutation rates should be. Rather than put you through that, let me provide you with some solid starting values:

- Population size set to 512

- Elitism rate set to 10%

- Crossover rate set to 70%

- Mutation rate set to 5%

- Maximum generations (number of evolutions) set to 2048

Depending on the speed of your computer, the programming language used to write the GA and a few other factors including the size of the backtest data, you may want to adjust these GA values. The population size and maximum generations will affect the total execution time of the GA simulation the most, so if you want to decrease the time it takes to run the simulation then you might want to lower these values first.

10.5 Summary

Before I close out this chapter, I want to share one last bit of advice with you. If you do decide to go down the path of using a GA simulation to come up with new trading strategies, please, **PLEASE** make sure you test it on a practice account first before you try using it with a live account. Do this for the first few strategies you generate in order to adjust the GA simulation accordingly.

Do not forget to use a good risk management strategy such as the one outlined in Section 6.2. It can be tempting to just use a new strategy blindly because the great returns it had. You may even be tempted to increase your risk in the hopes of higher returns. Be careful what you wish for, you may get those larger returns initially, but large losses are also just waiting to happen.

I'm a huge fan of using GAs for Forex trading strategies. Admittedly they are more complex than a strategy you execute "by hand", however they do take a lot of emotion out of everyday trading. In my personal opinion, this benefit far outweighs the complexity.

In the final part of the book I will walk you through some personal experiences. The main reason for me writing this book was to share my experiences and try to ensure people do not necessarily follow the same path of frustration that I had. Ah, the good old days.

Part III

Sitting In The Shade Of The Tree

CHAPTER 11

In The Beginning - My Early Attempts

When I first started trading the Forex markets, I had no idea what I was doing. At the beginning of the book I mentioned that I stumbled across the Forex by watching a children's cartoon show. Funny as it seems, that is actually what happened! I remember it very well. I was watching Disney's Recess on TV with my wife. I wish I could say that I was watching the show with my kids, but they weren't born yet. I've always been a cartoon fan, and this one seemed to strike the right chord with me. I'm going to go on record and say I was watching it to find appropriate cartoons for my yet-to-be-born children.

The episode in question was called "The Coolest Heatwave Ever[1]". One of the characters was talking about a ski trip he had taken with his father that quickly turned into a chase to stop a villain who wanted

---

[1]Season 5, Episode 1

to bring down "world currency markets" as his evil plot. The "smart" character in the group gasped and said that doing so would have brought the world economy to a halt and how it was wonderful it was that this other character and his father were successful in stopping the villain.

For whatever reason the concept of "world currency markets" caught my attention. I honestly wasn't sure if this was just some plot point that was added for the sake of the story, or something else. At the time I was looking for ways to supplement my income via investments yet all I knew of were the standard mutual funds. I grew to dislike and distrust mutual funds after watching countless friends and family members lose their income sources because of market crashes and the like. Most people would just tell them to ride out the storm, except for the fact that most of them were retired and this "storm" was digging into their livelihood.

At the time I was reading about stock trading and a few other topics related to personal finance, but nothing really struck a chord with me. I had traded a few stocks myself, but the fees associated with each trade were high when compared to the paltry profits I was making. I traded in companies I understood, companies I worked for (being painful aware of insider trading laws and such) and it was fun. I made some money, but hardly enough to make a living from it. I hated the fees associated with every trade - these fees made me feel as if I was being punished for trying to take control of my own finances. Also after being caught up in the tech bubble of the early 2000s, I was painfully aware how easy it is to lose money on the stock market if you are not prepared. All of these things made me curious as to what this "world currency market" was and how it worked.

After a bit of searching on the Internet, I found out that it was called the *foreign exchange market*, and it was huge. I grew quite excited and figured I had found a great way to make some money on the side! It seemed similar enough to stocks that I was confident that I could pick this up quickly. I loved the extended hours, the leverage (free money!) and the lack of fees for every trade! It seemed to be exactly what I was looking for.

I had the dream most of us do when we are young, namely to strike it rich as quickly as possible! Everything else would work itself out later. I viewed trading the Forex as a way to make that happen, so I started the same way most anyone would - I opened up a demo account with the first broker I found in my Google search.

11.1 Forex Trading For Fun

To be fair, I did read some more and learned the basics of how the Forex worked. I loved the idea of a demo account, since I was still painfully aware of how easy it is to lose money on the stock market if you don't know what you're doing. The broker I used started me with $100,000$ USD for my demo account and no real guidance, which was fine by me. I was reading books and blogs, tutorials and YouTube videos. The concept seemed simple enough that I had the confidence that only a fool knows, so I jumped in and started trading currencies on my demo account.

I liked my Forex broker's trading platform and order system. Both of them seemed intuitive and simple to use. The trading platform was definitely a lot better than the system my stock broker had. Then again, I still harbored resentment towards my stock broker. So it wasn't exactly a fair comparison. Still, my Forex broker let me buy and sell individual units of currency, which seemed to make more sense to me than trading using these *lots* that I was reading about. I liked this fine-grained control more.

My practice account came with a default leverage of 20:1. I knew a bit about leverage, but to be honest with you I didn't pay much attention to this in the material I was reading. I was more interested in seeing how well I could do by watching the charts. I decided to increase the leverage to 50:1 for no better reason than I thought it would help since I would have more money to trade with.

My first currency was the EUR/USD. It was popular, there was a lot of activity and it seemed "cool". However I was quickly overwhelmed with all the price updates happening so quickly. I also didn't expect to see a line chart showing the close price for the currency pair since it didn't match the candlestick charts that I was seeing in my Internet readings. I changed the line graph to candlesticks and life was good again.

I read up on candlestick charts a bit more since they were still new to me. My stock trading experience was limited to price watching and news alerts. I suppose I was more of a fundamental trader when it came to stocks, so I didn't see any reason aside from monitoring the current price for a stock. For the Forex, candlestick charts made sense to me, especially with so much volatility with the currency prices! I was reading about candlestick patterns, of which there were many, so I tried to focus on a few key ones such as the hanging man, morning and evening stars, spinning tops and engulfing lines. Combined with some trend spotting by "feel" for lack of a better term, I began trading my demo account. What came next should be no surprise to anyone.

I though what every new trader thinks - *I can make millions doing this!*

11.1.1 Early Success

With a few quick clicks of my mouse and my new found ability to spot trends without any type of technical indicator or trend line, I made $2,000 in the first week by occasionally watching the 5 minute chart and making some random trades using my own dysfunctional trading system. At the time I was mainly practicing my trading over my lunch break or in the few minutes I had in the morning before heading off to work. I would trade in the evening sometimes, but I didn't feel like the prices moved as much as I saw during the day, so I thought it simply wasn't worth my time given my successes during the day.

My trading system was very, very simple. I would notice a candlestick pattern like a bullish engulfing pattern and other times I noticed small trends in the candles themselves, essentially "eyeballing" the trend. It worked, and I was making some good trades. I was trading infrequently enough that my losses were few and far between. I was making short trades, jumping in and out of trades quickly in order to score a quick profit.

Let me be absolutely clear - I was, for all intents and purposes, scalping the market. Not only was I scalping, I was doing it in a dangerous way. I was not using any technical indicators, I was simply looking at trends made by the candlesticks and trying to spot a candlestick pattern or two in order to justify my trades. My new found gains were made based on a few pips of profit for each trade, usually between 1 to 5 pips each. If I ever reached 10 pips profit, well that was a very good trade indeed!

I also ended up babysitting each trade, usually only having an order open for anywhere from a few minutes to no more than an hour or two before closing it out. I was using upwards of 30% - 50% of my account balance for each trade, so this babysitting seemed worth it given how heavily invested I was in each trade. The profits were good, and it seemed like I was making more money in 15 minutes than I was for an entire week of work. I was getting excited, and I was already dreaming of vacation properties I would own and the trips around the world I would take.

11.1.2 The Joys Of Math

I started paying attention to the rate of return I was seeing. It worked out to roughly 2%, which is not great compared to other investments, but I had managed to get that 2% *in a week*! That's definitely better than any other investments available from my bank or past financial planners I had worked with!

I reasoned that I could easily hit this return each day if I actually focused on what I was doing rather than just the few minutes per day that I was trading now. Compounding that 2% return on a daily basis made my head hurt in terms of the new found wealth I was about to fall into. A simple $1,000 investment with a 2% compounded daily return would net me $115,888.74 within a year[2]! Oh let the good times roll! I knew I could do it, I just needed to try!

I calculated in my head out how much I wanted to make before I quit my job. Three million dollars was a nice round number to me, and one that I was satisfied with. I would stop trading, just go with

---

[2]Assuming 240 trading days per year.

a low interest investment and live comfortably. I figured I could get that much in just over 3 years if I could successfully maintain a 2% daily return.

I reasoned with myself that I would have bad days, but I was convinced that the 2% figure was so small that I could easily exceed it by 1 or 2% more for the days following a bad day so I could easily average this rate of return. Did I mention that I was star struck with my amazing abilities to trade the Forex with no real knowledge? As you can imagine, reality gave me a wakeup call, just not right away.

11.2 Going Live

By the time I had decided to start trading with my own money, I had been practicing more regularly on my practice account. By more regularly I mean that I would try to spend a few more minutes justifying my trades instead of just floating by. I would purposefully look for trends over longer time periods and I was more careful when entering and exiting trades. I was very risk-adverse and closed trades out early just to get the smallest profit. A lot more babysitting, but at the same time a lot fewer trades.

It worked out in the longer run. After about 2 months I ended up making just over $20,000 on my practice account. I was sure I knew what I was doing. I would casually tell my wife: "Yeah, so I made another $500 today while trading Forex," as if it was nothing. I had fully convinced myself that I knew what I was doing. It was time to open a live account.

11.2.1 Trading Exotics - Enter The USD/ZAR

During the time with my practice account I had switched to trading the USD/ZAR, which is the US Dollar/South African Rand pair. I was studying artificial intelligence via correspondence with the University of South Africa (UNISA) at the time, so I felt good using this pair.

If you have never traded the USD/ZAR, then I wouldn't recommend it at all. There is very little trade volume and the spreads are massive. At the time the USD/ZAR had a spread that ranged from 45 to 300(?!) pips[3]. Combine the spread with the wild price changes experienced by this pair and you can wipe out your account quite quickly.

Of course at this time I knew nothing of what the spread meant, nor did I care. I was successful! I made more than 20% in returns in a few short months on my practice account! So I did what anyone else in my position would do. I invested some of my own money and I went live.

11.2.2 The Initial Investment

I started small - I opened my first live account with $1,000 and an expectation that I could double this initial investment within a few weeks. I was excited!

Now I was no fool, and I remembered the one golden rule you must follow for any type of medium to high risk investment:

Never invest more money than you are willing to lose.

$1,000 is not a lot of money when you are talking about investments, but it is a lot of money for most of us to essentially "throw

---

[3]My broker at the time had a variable spread for their pairs.

away". Regardless, that was what I was willing to risk and by my calculations I really didn't need more than that. After all, I managed to make 20% in just over two months on my demo account. How could things possibly go wrong?

11.2.3 Chaos Ensues

My first live trade was a nightmare. I literally checked it every minute to see how it was going. I started watching the 5 second chart just to get as close to real-time as I could get in terms of looking for trends to make sure my trades were profitable. I did not have my emotions under control. In fact, I was absolutely panic stricken! Yet just the day before I was having no problem putting up to $50,000 of leveraged funds into a single trade.

My first trade was worth $400 when I opened it. By the time I closed it out I ended up with a $50 loss. This repeated a few times until I was down about $125 that first day of live trading. To put it bluntly I was out of my mind. Panic set in *very* quickly and I ended up breaking every single rule I had, which is pretty sad considering I didn't have many to begin with. I didn't look for candlestick patterns, I simply looked for obvious trends on the candlestick chart I was watching. I had the brilliant mis-conception that if I could watch the 5 minute chart for my practice account, then the 5 second chart would be that much better at confirming my trends. Yeah, I was clearly out of my head.

I waited about 3 days before trying to trade again. The first thing I decided was that smaller trades would be safer - and they were. I ended up gaining about $50 in the following week of trades. I was only risking about 10 - 15% of my principle for each trade, a far cry from the 30 - 50% I was using previously.

Overall I was still down, but it was a better experience. Once I got into a rhythm I was feeling much better and far less anxious. That is until the spreads caught up with me. My risk:reward ratio was somewhere around 4:1 at the best of times, since I also had a bad habit of changing my SL and TP levels haphazardly based on my interpretation of the charts at any given time.

I was still trading the USD/ZAR, which is notorious for wild price swings. I was caught up in a few of those volatile price swings the following week and ended up with another losing week. In order to counteract this loss due to volatility I did what every sane new Forex trader does - I increased my SL level and made my risk:reward ratio much, much worse. At the absolute worse I had a risk:reward ratio of 10:1, which I justified by exiting my trades early to make a meager profit. Yet when the price swings didn't swing back, I ended up losing all my gains and then some.

After about a month I stopped trading altogether. I had lost $775 from my original $1,000 investment and I was bruised and bloodied mentally as well as financially. Clearly I had much to learn.

11.3   Hitting The Books

I had a few Forex books and websites that I was reading before I started, but now I decided to go back and really read them properly, looking for tips and techniques. A lot of what I was reading made everything look so easy: charts that gave perfect patterns, trend lines that never failed, other technical indicators like Fibonacci Retracements that seemed to spin gold. My inner skeptic started to come out and flash the big red warning lights, but I did not listen closely enough. Dollar signs were in my eyes again! I attributed my failures to not using these techniques in my trading, so I clearly just had to follow these recipes to be successful.

I love to read, so I bought more books on trading the Forex and read them one after the other. I even invested in a $300 "Forex Beginners" course that came on 4 DVDs. Yet something was still nagging at me while I was reading these books and watching these videos. They all seemed to be geared towards traders coming from the stock market who wanted to try Forex, or for those Forex traders who were trying to get to the next level, but they weren't really useful to a new trader such as myself. Lots of them were marketed at beginners, but they just didn't seem to strike the right chord with me. Concepts and terms I had never heard of were being thrown around with little explanation, which bothered me to no end. Things have changed since then, but I still felt a little frustrated with them. The "Forex Beginners" course that I bought had a similar pattern as the books. The indicators seemed to line up just perfectly with the charts, so again I began to believe that the problem was that I just wasn't using the right tools-of-the-trade in my day-to-day trading activities.

I went back to my demo account and tried to apply what I had learned, and that's when the frustration started to kick in. It seems I could never apply those indicators to my charts correctly and find those ideal entry points! For whatever reason, the indicators and charts simply did not line up for me! This was an incredibly demoralizing experience, and I honestly started to shun the advice in these books and videos. *Charlatans and witchcraft* I thought to myself, there is no

227

way that these indicators actually work! Yet the reasoning behind the indicators seemed sound, so I didn't want to abandon them completely.

One of my character traits is that I'm stubborn. I didn't want to give up on these indicators because they didn't work for me, so I started using different time frames for my charts. The further out I went, the better these indicators lined up. It turns out that a lot of these books not only had different time periods for the different indicators, they also had different currency pairs! The charts they were using didn't exactly make this clear, but once I spotted the differences between charts in the same book, I started to feel better about my own failure to use these indicators.

It's usually at this point that people give up on Forex trading. They trade, they lose, they read and fail to apply the indicators properly or they use too many at once and get conflicting signals. Forex trading can be as easy or as hard as you want it to be, but you must respect it or it will take you for a ride and leave you with no money to show for it. I refused to let this happen to me and I continued on, stubborn as ever.

Perseverance certainly paid off! I started to see gains again while my frustrations dwindled. Not everything was perfect, but at least I could properly apply these tools to my own trades. It was then that I realized I had to revisit a lot more than just the tools I was using to decide when to make my trades.

11.3.1 Refining My Strategy

Revisiting my practice account, I reset the balance I had available in the account. I decided that $100,000 was an unrealistic account balance, since I was not going to be investing that much anytime soon. My reasoning was that the amount was so great, I couldn't realistically trade it with emotion since I was not at a point in my life where I would have invested that much. So I reset my account to $1,000 and I continued to read, watch and learn as much as I could while trading on this account. I continued on my practice account for a few months before I dared to go back to a live account again. I learned to treat my practice account like a live account, learning to keep my emotions in check. I thought I had done that before, but clearly that wasn't the case.

I stopped trading the USD/ZAR and switched back to the EUR/USD. While there was a lot more activity with the EUR/USD, it was far less volatile in terms of price fluctuations. I started being more conservative with my money management and never risked more than 10% of my account balance on any single trade. It was still aggressive, but not nearly as bad as it once was. I also stopped changing my SL and TP triggers after my orders were placed. I would still close orders early if necessary, but I didn't change these levels unnecessarily as I had done so in the past.

I started using larger time frames, going from the 5 minute chart to a 15 or 30 minute chart instead. Sometimes I toyed with the 1 or 4 hour charts as well, but I kept going back to the 15 minute chart. I still liked the shorter time frames, since I was still a fan of shorter trades. I was much closer to a day trader than a scalper now. It certainly made me feel better and I started re-kindling that excitement I had when I first discovered the Forex.

I was slowly honing my trading skills and I was overcoming my fears of trading live again. I began to understand what I didn't fully understand, and it put me into a content place since it forced me

229

to accept my own limitations. I realized that making millions wasn't going to happen overnight. With that understanding, I decided I was ready to give it another shot.

11.4 Live Trading Redux

I went back to my live account and topped it up to $500 this time, determined not to make the same mistake again. I stuck with the EUR/USD and I started trading the moving average crossovers.

After about 3 months I was up about 10%, which was head-and-shoulders above the best I could have hoped for as I floundered like a fish with my previous attempt at live trading. I was happy to be making money, and I felt vindicated. I changed my leverage from 50:1 to 30:1 and brought my risk:reward ratio down to 3:2. It wasn't the best approach, but it was better than the 10:1 ratio I had before! I also lowered the amount I was trading to 10 - 15% of my account balance. I hadn't learned about the 2% rule yet, but that would come later in my Forex readings. I would still strongly recommend new traders stick to the 2% rule as it will keep you afloat for a lot longer while you get your bearings for live trading.

Yes, things were a lot better now, but as I found out over time, old habits are hard to break.

11.4.1 Old Habits Die Hard

Even though my emotions were not getting the best of me as they did when I first started, I noticed I still had the urge to check my trades whenever I had a free moment. I still had pangs of fear when I placed a trade via my live account. After a year of live trading I realized that

I was never going to completely erase this fear. I screwed up pretty bad when I started, and those scars were going to take a long time to heal.

I had to do something that would separate me from my emotions completely. I was holding steady in my trades, but I noticed I was starting to have more losing trades than winning ones. My SL triggers were working as expected, but I was still slowly loosing money.

In hindsight, I realize I needed to re-think my strategy, but it wasn't clear to me then. No, at the time I attributed these losses to my emotions getting the better of me and so, I began to second guess myself. I knew this was a slippery slope so I decided it was time to take another small break from live trading and to do what I do best - write code.

Chapter 12

Enter The Automaton

I'll be the first to admit that I'm stubborn. Another character trait of mine is I'm lazy. In fact, I'm so lazy that I will work incredibly hard to make sure I don't have to do something a second time if I can help it. That's how I viewed trading the Forex. Placing trades were an emotional activity I didn't like doing, so I wanted to work hard and automate the process so I wouldn't have to do it again.

An *automaton* is defined to be a moving mechanical device that imitates a human being. I realized I needed to keep my emotions in check when making trades, so I decided to write an automated trading agent. It would also help me never have to trade by hand again, which was a worthy, if somewhat unrealistic, goal. Let me explain how I wrote my first automated trading system.

12.1 Automating My Forex Trading

I am a programmer by profession. I have written all kinds of applications for a all kinds of industries, so naturally I thought I should be able to write a program to help me trade the Forex.

The broker I was using at the time had a programmatic interface to their trading system, also known as an API, which allowed me to mimic what I could do on the platform myself. That helped with my decision to make an automated trading system, since otherwise it would have been quite a difficult task to automate my trades.

Not all brokers offer an API to trade on their platform and those that do often have conditions on who has access to them. Some brokers require a minimum deposit while others have a monthly fee. The minimum deposit requirement is the more common of the two, with the minimum required balance ranging from $5,000 USD to as high as $100,000. My personal broker offers a monthly fee that is discounted depending on how much leveraged trade volume is traded per month, so it is possible to use their API without any monthly cost.

If you seriously want to get into automated trading, you can do so in a few different ways. Depending on your skill level and how far you want to go with your automated trading agent, I would recommend researching the different brokers early and include an API in your criteria. It may limit your list of available brokers, but it will save you some frustrations later on.

The concept was simple, I just wanted to replicate what I was doing manually. So off I went, constructing a very simple trading agent that would look for a moving average crossover and trade it when certain conditions would be met. In my manual trading, I learned that placing a trade right when the moving averages crossed over was a bad idea. There were times when the market was moving in a sideways fashion, which in turn caused a lot of "false" crossovers which caused me lots of losses due to the spread. That's when I realized one of the conditions I needed was some sort of *delta* value that the two moving averages needed before I would act on a new crossover.

I had learned from previous mistakes and I tested and tuned the application on a practice account and not with a live account. It was a slow process since I was essentially trading "live", but with a practice account. It meant that if I wanted to test a weeks worth of data, I had to wait a week for the data to come through my practice account. I knew this would never scale, especially if I wanted to test out new strategies. I needed another approach that sped up this process.

12.2   Imitating The Broker

So what was an aspiring automated Forex trader to do? I automated my broker of course! I wrote a simple application to act like my broker, and provide me with data I could use to test strategies against. Since I controlled this *mock broker*, I could control the speed of the data feed to my strategies. I was no longer tied to real-time data, meaning I could test a weeks worth of trading data in a few seconds!

There were some subtle differences between my mock broker and my real broker. My mock broker did not have variable spreads for starters. It also could not serve more than one currency pair at a time. I added an awful lot of functionality to help me mimic my broker, from specifying different leverage options to handling margin calls. I also added the ability to track my account balance, let me know how many units were available for an order, keep track of what orders were open, and maintain a record of closed orders. Other things included handling SL and TP triggers as well as being able to open and close orders on demand, which was useful when I wanted to test what would happen if I closed an order myself rather than wait for the application to do it for me.

It certainly was more complex than just being a dumb funnel of currency pair data as I first envisioned the problem to be. Yet it was the data feed functionality that was one of the biggest issues. I had a broker that would allow me to open and close orders, but it was not capable of giving me any pricing data that I could use to actually *test* my program.

12.3 Finding Data For Backtesting

Backtesting is a term used to describe running historic data for a currency pair through a trading system in order to test the trading system to see how a given strategy performs. It's a common approach used by most traders, and a lot of trading platforms support it. Unfortunately for me, my broker's platform did not. This is part of the reason I wrote my mock broker, but it was missing a key piece. I still needed the historic data to run through it!

While I had a mock broker I could use to test strategies, I needed to find more historic data I could use to test those strategies with! To this point, all the data I had was what I had skimmed from my broker's

APIs, which wasn't nearly enough. I wanted a few years worth of data in order to really test my strategies.

I searched the Internet and found someone who sold historic tick data for all the major currency pairs and offered it on multiple DVDs for a fair price. I paid around $200 USD for 10 years worth of historic tick-by-tick[1] data. I tested with this data for nearly a month as I worked on new strategies, all the while looking for something that gave me an edge. Since I wasn't satisfied with my old crossover strategy, I needed to find something new. This "something new" was essentially the same moving average crossover, but with different period sizes for the moving average indicators as well as a new delta value.

Once I was confident of my impending success, I dove back into the backtesting! My strategies didn't work at first, so I tweaked them bit by bit using the historic data for EUR/USD. I continued to refine the system and constantly backtesting it against a years worth of historic data until I was getting great returns. I had made approximately 150% in returns over a year using the historic data! To say I was pleased would be putting it mildly!

I was excited, so I decided to try it right away. I fought the urge to put it on my live account right away and instead I let it run on my practice account for a week. Thank goodness I did, since I could never have imagined the results I saw. Not only did my new trading system not work like it did when I was backtesting it, it ended up losing money faster than if I had randomly chosen when to buy or sell!

---

[1]Tick data is essentially the real-time price changes for a given currency pair.

12.3.1 What Went Wrong

I fell into two traps while backtesting this new strategy. The first was I was over-fitting my solutions to the test data. What this means is I was constantly updating my strategy to fit my test data, which is great if history repeats itself exactly. Unfortunately, that never happens, so my strategies worked well *for a specific period in time*. Testing against any other data meant the strategy didn't work at all. It is possible that had I let it run for longer it would have picked up, but the losses were so drastic (nearly 70% of all the trades were losing trades) I couldn't justify letting it run longer than a week.

The second trap I fell into was the test data was absolute garbage! There were holes in the data and most of the data itself seemed wrong. What I mean is there was very little movement in the EUR/USD price data during peak hours, when I would have expected to see a lot of price fluctuation. I accounted for different timezones that might have put the data at the wrong hour or over a weekend, but it seemed pretty consistent in terms of it staying pretty steady. I have no idea where this data was sourced from, but it was clear it was either not done correctly or it was simply bad data. Plotting the data helped visualize what it looked like, and it was clear there were some reliability issues with this data.

Again I searched for historic data I could test with. The Meta-Trader platform from MetaQuotes offers the ability to download historic data, but I found massive holes in the data spanning weeks at a time, so that was not an option. Shorter-term ranges were more reliable (a few weeks at a time) but not the range that I was hoping for (at least a years worth of data). After much searching I found that my own broker did offer accurate historic data for free. There were two catches with this data however; a minimum account balance was required to access the data and the data only covered the major pairs and none of the exotics. I was fine with both these conditions. After my experience with USD/ZAR, I swore off the exotics for trading. I also had enough in my account to access the data. I took this new data and ran with it.

12.3.2 When In Doubt, Plot!

One drawback of using a mock broker is you don't always get to see what the strategies look like. On a broker's platform, you have charting tools to see how the indicators look against the currency pair data across different time frames, but my mock broker lacked this ability. It had no interface, just an engine running in the background spitting out some messages to the screen. My new data was giving me good returns, and testing it on the demo data showed some initial success. Yet I was still bothered by the lack of any plots for my backtested data. By plotting these indicators against the historic data, I could see exactly how they did, and did not, work.

I spent a good chunk of time trying to come up with different ways of plotting my trading system. I tried spreadsheets, custom charting libraries, and other techniques to plot my indicators against the data. Spreadsheets didn't work well because I could never figure out how to have multiple plots at the same time, and it honestly didn't work out very well especially with larger data sets. I then used a charting library to plot my own charts. This worked but the libraries were often buggy or poorly documented, so I would run into frustrating errors that nobody seemed to know how to fix.

In the end I used a program called *gnuplot* to make my charts with the indicators. There was a bit of a learning curve, but once I figured it out, it was a huge help. My charts were pretty ugly, missing date labels and a few other things you would see in normal charting software, but it was prefect for my needs. I was able to visually see my indicators and how they worked when applied to my historic data. This is something I still do to this day, and I strongly recommend you learn how to plot your own strategies against historic data. It's a great way to look for inconsistencies such as missing data, price data that is "flat" and has no variation. Find a technique that works for you and stick with it. It will certainly help you in the long run, since it is a lot easier to see when your strategy is over-fitting your training data or not by looking at the technical indicators to see if they fit too perfectly with the training candlestick data.

A few months of trading with this latest strategy (at the time) was successful. I was making a 2 - 5% return each quarter, but after about 3 months I found I had to adjust my strategy slightly to continue my trend. I knew there had to be a better way, which is when it dawned on me. Why not create a trading system that evolves? That's when I decided to put my trading system up on blocks and start to re-write it to use genetic algorithms instead.

12.4   Growing Strategies

I had always wanted to introduce some level of AI into my trading strategies, but I struggled with figuring out *how* I wanted to do it. Neural networks were finicky, and expert systems were too convoluted for the types of strategies I was using. Then it dawned on me - genetic algorithms were a near perfect fit for my particular strategies.

I began reading about genetic algorithms a few years ago, and I immediately fell in love. There was something elegant about their simplicity I found alluring. They also seemed like the perfect choice for allowing my trading strategy to evolve.

I covered a lot of my strategies using GAs for evolving my trading system back in Chapter 10, so I won't repeat them here. I still find bugs in the system to this day, but as I said previously, plotting the "solutions" helps a lot. When I first started using GAs I was more focused on getting the GA code to work than plotting its solutions, which of course led to some *interesting* bugs.

I recall one particularly funny bug where I had mis-coded my simulation engine by re-running the GAs training data as the test data for the GA. Basically the test data for the strategy I had just found was run against the same data that I used to come up with that same strategy. When that happens, hilarity ensues.

Do you know what happens when you find an ideal strategy for some currency data and then run that strategy on the exact same data? I do. Starting with $1,000, I made over *one billion dollars* while backtesting the solution over a year's worth of data! Oh I was puzzled for a moment or three, but I knew something was wrong. Secretly I hoped nothing was wrong and I was already starting to formulate how quickly I was going to get this into my live account to get things rolling. Still, as Occam's Razor states, the simplest answer is most often the correct one.

What happened was the GA's fitness function was set to find the maximum profit for the training data and I had set my backtest to re-train once every 3 days. Since I was then using the *same* training data to test each strategy, the strategy always fit the data perfectly thus producing amazing results. It was good for a short laugh, but I felt like a fool for letting it happen. The lesson I learned that day was to question all my results, regardless of how well or how poorly they performed.

12.4.1 Was Darwin Right?

Obviously I have stuck with using GAs to come up with strategies for my trading system. So how does it compare with my old system? Quite well actually! The two systems are drastically different, with my original strategy using fixed period sizes looking for moving average crossovers with nothing more than a delta and the new system adding an RSI indicator to help confirm or deny these strategies. It is an apples-to-oranges comparison and it could be argued either way in terms of what is a better strategy.

Looking at raw numbers, my original, inflexible trading system was reasonably making in the range of $2 - 5\%$ return per quarter, while my new GA-based trading system is netting an average quarterly return between $5 - 9\%$. While the returns are impressive, there are good quarters and there are bad quarters. Of course this is why diversification is so important, since you want to be able to weather these inconsistencies.

Looking at the raw numbers it seems the GA-based system is the better of the two. I would agree, but for different reasons. To me the biggest advantage is I don't feel like I need to babysit my strategy like I had to in the past. I still keep an eye on it, but I don't need to adjust it every few months. There were a lot of factors I had to be careful of when writing the GA version of my trading strategy, but

I firmly believe it was worth it. Trading the Forex is a major part of growing my money tree and moving to a GA-based trading strategy plays a major role in its success.

CHAPTER 13

The Zen Of Tree Growing

Growing a money tree is fun and frustrating at the same time. My early attempts to find immediate wealth through trading the Forex were not successful, but to be fair I was also rushing headlong into it without understanding what I was getting myself into. I learned from my mistakes, adapted my strategies and used existing skills to hone my trading strategies. I learned that it wasn't about immediate wealth, it was about growing wealth steadily and reliably. As I covered in Chapter 7, diversification should be used to nurture and grow your money tree.

When I first started taking control of my own investments, I used two simple options: savings bonds and mutual funds. Now I have diversified quite a bit by dropping the mutual funds, adding dividend-earning stocks that have a dividend reinvestment plan (DRIP) and, of course, trading the Forex market. I continue to purchase savings bonds since I like their patriotic symbolism and low-risk nature.

Now that my money tree is growing, I want to pause for a moment and wax philosophical as I reflect on how I got here. This chapter is more about the lessons I have learned over these past 10 years on my journey, with the hopes of helping you find out where to focus your own energies, in order to help you grow *your* money tree.

13.1   Build A Budget

I wish I had learned this lesson earlier in my life: a budget is essential for success in growing a money tree. It is next to impossible to live from the fruit of a money tree without knowing what your financial needs are. Budgets can also help you avoid acquiring "bad debt" by ensuring you only spend what you have and don't rely on credit cards for "impulse purchases" or use them as a crutch to get by.

When people think of a budget, a few things often come to mind: a whole lot of receipts, a notebook, a spreadsheet and absolute chaos. It doesn't have to be that difficult, and budget software has come a long way. I use a program called *You Need A Budget (YNAB)*[1], which is the only one I would recommend for anyone who, well, needs a budget! It is simply an outstanding application, incredibly easy to use and very user friendly. They also have mobile versions for most smart phones that synchronizes with your computer, so you don't have to carry a bunch of receipts around. I absolutely love it.

Budgets are personal; no one is going to judge you by what you put in your budget except yourself. If you want to be successful in growing a money tree, you must make a budget **and stick to it**! I have a reminder setup to update my budget every Monday night. This entire process takes me about 15 - 30 minutes, depending on

---

[1]http://www.youneedabudget.com/

how many transactions I have from the previous week. It's not a very time consuming process, and does help make sure that I stay on track with my finances. Budgets are critical to maintaining the health of a money tree. Without one (or worse, without sticking to one), you risk having your money tree wither up and die because it won't be able to sustain your needs.

The first time I wrote up my budget, it was a living hell. I felt so paranoid, frustrated, anxious and I was a "big ball" of emotion that it literally took me *three days* to get all my bills and receipts together in order to plan out my initial budget. It wasn't that these things were difficult to find, I just had to control my anxiety and calm myself down to pull it all together and just get it done. Once I was done, I felt *a lot* better.

One of the reasons I didn't want to do the budget in the first place was that I suffered what most people do, the "I-know-what-I'm-doing-and-how-I-spend-my-money" syndrome. I knew exactly how much I was spending and that I was on track! I wasn't in any dire-straights financially, so why was I so anxious about writing down a budget? It was simple - I was afraid I was wrong. Turns out I was. My budget showed that I was overspending in a few areas like groceries, restaurants and general expenses. I was shocked, especially with the groceries! This was one area I could have sworn I had under control! Turns out that those small trips to the store to pick up "one-off" items added up quite quickly. Being conscious of this fact helped save $200 a month.

Creating a budget was the biggest step towards finding financial freedom for me. I strongly recommend that you build yourself a budget *before* you start growing your money tree.

13.2 Exploring New Strategies

When I first started to trade the Forex, I thought I had found the perfect tool to guide me on the path to financial freedom. The concept of a money tree wasn't fully formed in my mind yet, so I just looked at the Forex as a means to making some quick cash. I thought to myself *Why, no other investment is worth holding! The Forex can make me a millionaire overnight!*

I, of course, failed in this quest but my early failures taught me valuable lessons. Trading the Forex wasn't going to make me wealthy by itself. It had great potential to make money, but it was too volatile to think I could make a steady income from it. My father has been known to say "Every school costs money." You were right Dad, the Forex cost me money, especially in the early days. Once I managed to trade the Forex somewhat successfully, I started to think about other investment options and strategies. I kept an ear open and tried to understand what other people were doing. I determined that there is no single strategy that will make you wealthy and that diversification was key to being successful. I knew I needed to diversify, the only question was how to do it.

13.2.1 The Devil You Know

I never did fully divest myself from mutual funds and savings bonds when I started Forex trading. I understood these investment options well enough and I didn't want to completely divest myself from them. I suppose you could say I was an "optimistic pessimist" after my first few failures early in my Forex trading career. In reality my reasons for sticking with these options may have been in part due to some laziness and the rigmarole associated with cashing out of these investments and paying the associated penalties.

Over time I grew weary of mutual funds and their lack of progress, so I divested from them and moved to a DRIP strategy instead. The returns may not be as high as the heydays of my mutual funds, but they certainly are a lot more steady in terms of returns over the years.

13.2.2 Finding DRIPs

I had some friends who were also venturing out into personal investment options and they were focusing on DRIP stocks, throwing out terms like DRIP, SPP and the like. I knew of dividend-earning stocks, but I hadn't paid them much heed. My past stock experience was literally limited to buying low, selling high.

I was curious though, so I started reading up on dividend stocks, DRIPs and what they entitled. I ended up reading the complete series of books by Derek Foster. I would recommend his work to anyone who wants to delve further into the topic of dividend stocks and strategies associated with them. Derek's writing is straightforward and easy to follow.

After reading as much as I could find on the topic of DRIPs, I quickly realized that the steady flow of dividend payments as well as re-investing those dividend payments was a great way to grow a strong cash flow. Combined with Forex trading, I realized that adding a DRIP strategy to my financial plan would certainly make it stronger and more resilient.

That's when it dawned on me - "financial plan" wasn't the right term, or rather it wasn't describing what I wanted my investments to be. I wanted something that will give me money regularly. I wanted money to grow on trees. *I wanted a money tree.*

13.3   Growing A Money Tree

Growing a money tree is about building up a passive, but stable, income source. Writing out my budget helped me to identify my monthly needs. From there I quickly realized that financial freedom was a lot closer than I thought! I saw an opportunity to spend more time with my family and less time going out to work for a living.

But even though I wanted to spend more time with my family, I decided that I wouldn't give up working completely. I still like the idea of working because I like to interact with other people. I would, however, want to work where I thought I would have some fun. So I added another goal: in addition to obtaining financial freedom, I would work as a Barista at my local Starbucks. How exactly was I going to do this? Trading the Forex was one way, but adding DRIPs and savings bonds helped. With all these choices, how was I going to diversify? What exactly are my ratios? Here's a quick breakdown of how I am now growing my money tree:

- 35% in Forex

- 40% in dividend stocks that offer a DRIP

- 15% in savings bonds

- 10% in cash

There is a symbiotic relationship between my Forex trading and my dividend stocks. I generally keep a fixed size pool of funds in my Forex pool but take any gains I make from this pool at the end of each month and purchase additional shares in my dividend stocks. I then use the InvestMete[2] method to calculate how much I invest in each of my dividend stocks. The article on the Motley Fool does a good job of explaining it but the gist of the method is that you invest more into companies that are struggling while investing less in companies that are doing well. This is based on comparing the current stock price to its 52-week high and low. I like this method since it has been shown to actually increase returns rather than spreading out funds equally amongst the different stocks.

So how long does this method actually take? Roughly an hour a month, give or take. Around the 15th of each month I take a look at my Forex account and withdraw my profits for that month. I then take note of my starting balance and track it in a spreadsheet for the next month. I use an online calculator to figure out the InvestMete ratios for my various DRIP stocks and spread my Forex gains amongst them. Cheques are then written and mailed to my transfer agents and some records are added to a spreadsheet. I send a few letters in the morning and I'm done for the month.

If I end up with a loss that month, I skip adding any funds to my DRIP stocks and instead invest into my Forex account to maintain a minimum level for my Forex account. There is some legwork involved, but it is still a far cry from a 40 hour work week.

13.4 "Difficult" Is A State Of Mind

Implementing a life-changing decision is hard. It doesn't help that western society re-enforces the need for "instant gratification," mean-

---

[2]http://www.fool.com/DRIPPort/1999/DRIPPort990727.htm

ing most of us lack the patience for long-term goals or rewards. We want success *now*, we want to win *now*, we want our rewards *now*. What often happens is that when we fail to get this instant gratification, we become discouraged and give up.

Reading any type of book, website or blog on investments and financial planning can be incredibly frustrating; all the terms that are thrown at you can give you a headache! Then there's all the other information about personal finance available from the Internet, friends, family and professionals you may be speaking with. Why would anyone in their right mind want to take their financial future in their own hands?! *How is anyone making a living by doing all of this?!*

It definitely takes a change in thinking to overcome the need for "instant gratification" when it comes to financial freedom. You need to have a goal you are striving for and a reason to continue to strive towards it. For me it was simple. My wife had given birth to twins after years of us trying to start our family. Watching these little babies grow, learn and explore the world around them was so exciting that it drove a desire deep inside me to spend as much time with them as possible. I needed a way to achieve this, but I had to work and make money in order provide for them.

That's when I decided that I had to take matters in my own hands. Saving for retirement was one thing, but my kids would be grown up and tired of me by then. I needed to take control and speed things up a bit. I really started to focus on my Forex trading a lot more and I started digging into other ways to make a living without having to work. To me, learning a few new terms, keeping some records and figuring out how to move money between some different investments was not difficult enough to dissuade me from pursuing my dream of

252

spending as much time with my family as possible.

Everyone is different, so what ever it is that drives you to seek financial independence may not be the same reasons as mine. That's fine. The point is that you have something that drives you. There will always be bumps on the road, but don't let them dissuade you! Keep your driving goal in mind and use it as motivation. Every time I thought I was going to quit because I had a string of bad trades or a problem with my transfer agent and I wanted to just give up, well, I would look at my kids and find that fire again.

Difficult truly is a state of mind. If the end reward is desirable enough, it will outweigh any frustrations you may face. Anger and frustration are often rooted in ignorance. This is not meant as an insult, it is just my reasoning as to why people want to give up so easily. Learn what you need to learn, come up with a plan and approach the problem slowly and systematically. Trees do not grow overnight, but when nurtured properly they root themselves strongly and live for centuries, bearing fruit for those who care for them. I grow my money tree as much for my children as I do for myself and I refuse to believe it is too difficult.

13.5 Pondering The Future

Whatever your reasons for wanting to grow a money tree, keep them in mind as you proceed. The road ahead can be difficult at times but that shouldn't dissuade you from following the path. Patience is a virtue, success is attainable, fear and frustration can easily be overcome if you are true to yourself and believe in what you are doing. The notion of an overnight success is alluring, but unrealistic. Make your plan, identify your budget and realize with great joy that you are much closer than you would expect!

With that, I want to close out by sharing with you exactly why I want to work as a Barista at Starbucks.

The answer is actually pretty simple - I like working **and** I like meeting new people. I remember going to a Starbucks drive-through for the first time and I actually had a conversation with the girl at the drive-through window. Why did she want to talk with me? Partly because my latte was going to take a while to prepare, but also because she could. It was somewhat surreal, but endearing at the same time.

That conversation struck a chord with me; I decided that once I could do whatever I wanted with my life one of those things would be to work at Starbucks. That short exchange was a wonderful experience for me and it still resonates with me to this day. The atmosphere at my local Starbucks is so inviting that to me, it seems like an ideal work environment. That and the coffee is pretty good too.

I wish you well, I wish you success and most importantly of all, I wish you find that which brings you contentment. Happy growing.

254

Bibliography

[1]   *Baby Pips.*
      2013.
      URL: http://www.babypips.com/.

[2]   *Canada Revenue Agency Income Tax Rates.*
      2013.
      URL: http://www.cra-arc.gc.ca/tx/ndvdls/fq/txrts-
      eng.html.

[3]   *Canadian DRIP Primer.*
      2012.
      URL: http://www.dripprimer.ca.

[4]   *Canadian Income Tax Calculator.*
      2012.
      URL: http://www.taxtips.ca/calculators/taxcalculator.
      htm.

[5]   Grace Cheng.

7 Winning Strategies for Trading Forex.
Harriman House, 2007.

[6]   *CMS Forex - Forex Glossary.*
2013.
URL: http : / / www . cmsfx . com / en / forex - education /
Forex-Glossary/.

[7]   James Dicks.
Forex Made Easy.
McGraw-Hill, 2004.

[8]   Derek Foster.
Stop Working Too You Still Can.
Foster, 2009.

[9]   Derek Foster.
The Lazy Investor.
Foster, 2007.

[10] David E. Goldberg.
Genetic Algorithms in Search, Optimization, and Machine Learning.
Addison-Wesley, 1989.

[11] Raghee Horner.
Thirty Days of Forex Trading.
Wiley, 2006.

[12] *Individuals by total income level, by province and territory.*
2012.
URL: http://www.statcan.gc.ca/tables-tableaux/sum-
som/101/cst01/famil105a-eng.htm.

[13]   *Investment Tax Rates.*
       2012.
       URL: http://www.taxtips.ca/personaltax/investing/
       investmentincometaxrates.htm.

[14]   *Investopedia.*
       2012.
       URL: http://www.investopedia.com/.

[15]   Jared F. Martinez.
       The 10 Essentials of Forex Trading.
       McGraw-Hill, 2007.

[16]   Louis B. Mendelsohn.
       Forex Trading Using Intermarket Analysis.
       Marketplace Books, 2006.

[17]   James Lauren Bickford Michael Duane Archer.
       The Forex Chartists Companion.
       Wiley, 2007.

[18]   John L. Person.
       Candlestick and Pivot Point Trading Triggers.
       Wiley, 2007.

[19]   Sue Ellen Haupt Randy L. Haupt.
       Practical Genetic Algorithms.
       Second.
       Wiley, 2004.

[20]   J. Welles Wilder.
       New Concepts in Technical Trading Systems.
       Trend Research, 1978.

[21]   Riccardo Poli William B. Langdon.
      Foundations of Genetic Programming.
      Springer, 2002.

Glossary

AI Artificial Intelligence.

Artificial Intelligence A branch of computer science dealing with the simulation of intelligent behavior in computers.

Ask Price The price a seller is willing to accept for a currency, also known as the offer price.

AUD The abbreviation for Australia's currency, the Australian dollar.

Backtesting The process of testing a trading strategy using existing historical data.

Barista A person who makes and serves coffee to the public.

Base Currency The first currency quoted in a currency pair.

Basis Point A unit that is equal to $1/100th$ of 1%.

Bear Market A market that is trending in a negative direction.

Bid Price The price a buyer is willing to pay for a currency.

Binary Encoding Encoding where every bit of data is represented with a 0 or a 1.

Broker An individual or firm that charges a fee or commission for executing buy and sell orders submitted by an investor.

Bull Market A market that is trending in a positive direction.

CAD The abbreviation for Canada's currency, the Canadian dollar.

Candlestick A chart element that displays the high, low, opening and closing prices for a security for a specific time period.

CDIC Canadian Deposit Insurance Corporation.

CHF The abbreviation for Switzerland's currency, the Swiss franc.

Chromosome A set of parameters which define a proposed solution to the problem that a genetic algorithm is trying to solve.

Close Price The final price at which a security is traded for a specific time period.

CPP Canada Pension Plan.

Crossover An operation used to vary the programming of two chromosomes from one generation to the next.

Currency Pair The quotation of the relative value of a currency unit against the unit of another currency in the foreign exchange market.

Day Trading The buying and selling of stocks, currencies or securities on the same day, on the basis of small, short-term price fluctuations.

Dividend A sum of money paid regularly by a company to its shareholders out of its profits or reserves.

DRIP Dividend Reinvestment Plan.

EI Employment Insurance.

Elitisim The process of taking the "best" chromosomes from one generation and copying them to the next generation, leaving them unchanged.

EMA Exponential Moving Average.

EUR The abbreviation for the European Union's currency, the euro.

Exotic Currency A currency with little liquidity and limited dealing, which is neither a major or minor currency.

Fitness The measure of success a given solution has for the problem that a genetic algorithm is trying to solve.

Foreign Exchange Market A form of exchange for the global decentralized trading of international currencies.

Forex A common term used to describe the Foreign Exchange Market.

Fundamental Analysis A method of evaluating a security that entails attempting to measure its intrinsic value by examining related economic, financial and other qualitative and quantitative factors.

GA Genetic Algorithm.

GBP The abbreviation for the United Kingdom's currency, the British pound sterling.

GDP Gross Domestic Product.

Gene The encoding of a solution, often stored as part of a chromosome.

Genetic Algorithm A search heuristic that mimics the process of natural evolution.

GIC Guaranteed Investment Certificate.

Gross Domestic Product The total market value of all the goods and services produced by a nation for a specified period of time.

High Price The highest price that a security is traded at for a specific time period.

Interval a space of time.

Investor Any person who commits capital with the expectation of financial returns.

JPY The abbreviation for Japan's currency, the Japanese yen.

Leverage The use of various financial instruments or borrowed capital, such as margin, to increase the potential return of an investment.

Limit Order An order placed with a brokerage to buy or sell a set number of shares at a specified price or better.

Long Position The buying of a security such as a stock, commodity or currency, with the expectation that the asset will rise in value.

Lot A standard trading term referring to an order of $100,000$ units.

Low Price The lowest price that a security is traded at for a specific time period.

MA Moving Average.

MACD Moving Average Convergence Divergence.

Margin A required amount to have in a deposit in order to purchase a currency on credit.

Margin Call Action taken by the broker/dealer to close a position when the amount in margin is less than required.

Market Order An order to buy or sell as close to instantly as possible at the best price available when the order is placed and received.

Market Rate The current quote price of a currency pair.

Mating Another term for Crossover.

Micro-Lot A currency trading lot size that is $1/100th$ the size of the standard lot of $100,000$ units.

Mini-Lot A currency trading lot size that is $1/10th$ the size of the standard lot of $100,000$ units.

Momentum The advancement of price action in one direction or another in agreement of an overall trend.

Money Tree A collection of passive and semi-passive income sources allowing for financial independence.

Moving Average The average closing price of a specified period.

Mutation A genetic operator used to maintain genetic diversity from one generation of a population of genetic algorithm chromosomes to the next.

Mutual Fund An investment vehicle that is made up of a pool of funds collected from many investors for the purpose of investing in securities such as stocks, bonds, money market instruments and similar assets.

NYSE New York Stock Exchange.

NZD The abbreviation for New Zealand's currency, the New Zealand dollar.

OHLC Open High Low Close.

Open Price The initial price at which a security is traded for a specific time period.

Order An investor's instructions to a broker or brokerage firm to purchase or sell a security.

Oscillator A technical analysis tool that is banded between two extreme values and built with the results from a trend indicator for discovering short-term over-bought or oversold conditions.

Overfitting A modeling error which occurs when a function is too closely fit to a limited set of data points.

P/L Profit/Loss.

Period Another name for an interval.

PIP Price Interest Point.

Pipette $1/10th$ of a PIP.

Population A collection of chromosomes.

Position The total net exposure in a given currency.

Price Interest Point The smallest measurable value for a currency pair.

Quote Currency The second currency quoted in a currency pair.

Ranging Market A market in which a currency exchange rate moves up and down between two well-established levels.

REIT Real Estate Investment Trust.

Resistance A technical price level which a currency pair has a hard time rising above.

RESP Registered Education Savings Plan.

RRSP Registered Retirement Savings Plan.

RSI Relative Strength Index.

Scalping A trading strategy that attempts to make many profits on small price changes.

Selection A process in which individual chromosomes are chosen from a population for later crossover.

Share (Stock) A type of security that signifies ownership in a corporation and represents a claim on part of the corporation's assets and earnings.

Short Position Action taken by the trader to sell a currency.

SL Stop Loss.

SMA Simple Moving Average.

SPP Stock Purchase Plan.

Spread The difference between the ask and bid price.

Stop Loss An order placed with a broker to sell a security when it reaches a certain price.

Support A technical price level which a currency pair has a hard time falling under.

Technical Analysis A method used to predict future price trends by analyzing historical data patterns.

TFSA Tax Free Savings Account.

Tick The minimum upward or downward movement in the price of a security.

TP Take Profit.

Trader An individual who engages in the transfer of financial assets in any financial market, either for themselves, or on behalf of a someone else.

Trend The general direction of the market broken down into an up-trend, downtrend or sideways trend.

Trigger An action that is performed when a security price reaches a particular level.

TSX Toronto Stock Exchange.

USD The abbreviation for the United States of America's currency, the US dollar.

Volitility A measure of price fluctuation.

Volume A measure of the level of trading activity.

Index